Journey To *Love*

10th Anniversary Edition

Janeen Michael

Trilogy Christian Publishers
A Wholly Owned Subsidiary of Trinity Broadcasting Network
2442 Michelle Drive
Tustin, CA 92780

Copyright © 2020 by Janeen Michael

All rights reserved, including the right to reproduce this book or portions thereof in any form whatsoever.

For information, address Trilogy Christian Publishing
Rights Department, 2442 Michelle Drive, Tustin, Ca 92780.
Trilogy Christian Publishing/ TBN and colophon are trademarks of Trinity Broadcasting Network.

For information about special discounts for bulk purchases, please contact Trilogy Christian Publishing.

Manufactured in the United States of America

Trilogy Disclaimer: The views and content expressed in this book are those of the author and may not necessarily reflect the views and doctrine of Trilogy Christian Publishing or the Trinity Broadcasting Network.

10 9 8 7 6 5 4 3 2 1

Library of Congress Cataloging-in-Publication Data is available.

ISBN 978-1-64088-699-5 (Print Book)
ISBN 978-1-64088-700-8 (ebook)

Scripture quotations marked (KJV) are from the King James Version of the Bible.

Unless otherwise noted, Scripture quotations are from the Holy Bible, New International Version, copyright © 1973, 1978, 1984 by the International Bible Society. Used by permission of Zondervan. All rights reserved.

The "(NIV)" and "New International Version" trademarks are registered in the United States Patent and Trademark Office by International Bible Society. Use of either trademark requires the permission of International Bible Society.

Scripture quotations taken from the New American Standard Bible® (NASB), Copyright © 1960, 1962, 1963, 1968, 1971, 1972, 1973, 1975, 1977, 1995 by The Lockman Foundation Used by permission. www.Lockman.org

Scripture quotations taken from the Amplified® Bible (AMPC), Copyright © 1954, 1958, 1962, 1964, 1965, 1987 by The Lockman Foundation
Used by permission. www.Lockman.org

Scripture quotations taken from the New Living Translation Bible (NLT) Copyright © Tyndale House Publishers. 2004. *Holy Bible: New Living Translation*. Wheaton, Ill: Tyndale House Publishers.

Scripture quotations are from The ESV® Bible (The Holy Bible, English Standard Version®), copyright © 2001 by Crossway, a publishing ministry of Good News Publishers. Used by permission. All rights reserved.

Previously published by Xulon Press as *Journey to Love*, ISBN 978-1-607791-572-0, copyright © 2009.

Some names of persons mentioned in this book have been changed to protect privacy; any similarity between individuals described in this book to individuals known to readers is purely coincidental.

Dedication

I dedicate this book, with my sincerest gratitude, to Christ. For it is only because of His love, that I am now found in His intimate embrace of safety and rest.

I am eternally grateful to you God, for my ***Journey To Love***, as I now sail each day upon the winds of Your Spirit of Peace.

Contents

Preface 9
Acknowledgments 11
Introduction 13
10 Years of *Journey To Love* 19

Chapter One: Selective Hearing 21
Chapter Two: Tag! You're It! 49
Chapter Three: Jump Already! 75
Chapter Four: In Over My Head! 97
Chapter Five: Let Me Help You! 119
Chapter Six: Spit Up Ashore 141
Chapter Seven: Heart and Song of the Matter 159
Chapter Eight: Watch Out! 183

"Journey Journal" 199
Bibliography 225
How to Know God 227

Preface

There was an unexplainable distance that I felt between God and me; the cold shoulder, the silent treatment. Having that space between us was so painful. It hurt in such a deeply profound way but that pain was the impetus to my *Journey to Love*. It provoked me in a way unlike any other that I'd previously experienced, to seek God.

I tried to close the distance through my own self-effort and as a result was beat, gagged, and burned-out. I didn't believe that God loved me because my life was so full of violating experiences and injury. Not believing that God loved me was the root of the problem, the pain, the distance, my issue.

To believe requires a measure of risk and risk makes you vulnerable. Vulnerability was the posture that I had to assume in order to hear God's affirming voice and unwavering promise that He did, in fact, unconditionally love me. But I did not want to be vulnerable because it was far too regularly associated with heartbreak and pain. Due to some violating experiences that I had, I was afraid to trust. Fear is a whale of a burden.

I couldn't see His love for me until I accepted His invitation for a piggyback ride. He longed to navigate me away from my fears, unbelief and issues. In the meantime, before I hopped aboard, I was waiting for God and expected Him to fix this distance thing between us only to discover that He was waiting on me.

God desires that there be no space between Him and His children—just transparent, raw and unashamed communion 24/7. He showed me His love for me and He escorted me along to the pathway to wholeness and freedom. He showed me His commitment to His children and His miraculously powerful ability to deliver us from anything that has tangled us up and drawn us away from His side. I pray this book helps to do the same for you.

> "Jesus loves me! This I know,
> For the Bible tells me so;
> Little ones to Him belong,
> They are weak but He is strong."
>
> By Anna Bartlet Warner (1860)

Acknowledgments

 I want to thank my new Trilogy Publishing family for their support. Their careful consideration and elevation of my ministry has sharpened my purpose and encouraged my heart. May their investment in me bear much fruit in the lives of countless others for the glory of God, as is consistent with the incredible legacy of faith that they have carried out for over forty years.

Introduction

Journey To Love

Where was my Love?

He said He'd be with me always. So why was my heart hurting from loneliness and weeping from the pain? Fear and unbelief disconnected me from my maker, my Love.

> There is no fear in love [dread does not exist]. But perfect (complete, full-grown) love drives out fear, because fear involves [the expectation of divine] punishment, so the one who is afraid [of God's judgment] is not perfected in love [has not grown into a sufficient understanding of God's love].
> 1 John 4:18 (AMPC)

"But without faith it is impossible to please him: for he that cometh to God must believe that he is, and that he is a rewarder of them that diligently seek him" (Hebrews 11:6, KJV).

When I accepted Jesus Christ as my personal Lord and Savior, I was heaven-bound for sure, but the intimate relationship, the closeness and affection that I so desperately longed to feel from God was sorely missing.

Surely I had to *do* something for that level of relationship with God; earn it somehow or beg for it—something! I couldn't believe that having Him close to me in such an intimate and personal way 24/7 would ever happen, though I craved it to the point of aching. Rejection and abandonment was all that I felt.

> "I will never leave thee, nor forsake thee." (Hebrews 13:5b, KJV).

> "…and, lo, I am with you always, even unto the end of the world." (Matthew 28:20b, KJV).

For years I lived with the disconnection between knowing God and consciously experiencing an intimate relationship with Him: meaningful connection and closeness. I could neither hear nor take His promise to be with me into my heart fully due to all of the circus noise and turmoil in my life.

> "Above all, taking the shield of faith, wherewith ye shall be able to quench all the fiery darts of the wicked." (Ephesians 6:16, KJV).

The season of craziness that I was going through was relentless and blinding because my spiritual battle shield was down. My fear and unbelief seemingly uncovered and exposed me to every cruel dart of unworthiness and guilt that the enemy hurled at me, hindering the truth of God's promise from sinking deep into my heart.

I can identify with the Hebrews sentiments when after more than 400 years of enslavement, Moses was sent to facilitate their deliverance from the grips of Pharaoh. The Hebrews were so disconnected from the truth and promises of God that they did not believe that their deepest hope for freedom from the cruel clutches of the Egyptians would ever be heard by God or ever come to pass. They were blinded by their tumultuous situation.

> Moses told the Hebrews that God said they would be set free,"...but they did not listen to him because of their discouragement and cruel bondage." (Exodus 6:9b, NIV).

Not believing that God loved me was the root of my problem; the pain; the distance; my issue.

I believed God dealt with me only because He was obligated to do so as my Maker. Oh the questions that pile up on the heart and mind that cruelly beat you down when you believe you're being *tolerated*, in what should otherwise be an excitedly passionate, committed relationship.

The depth of embarrassment and shame that I tried to keep hidden was tormenting and wearisome; God's secret unwanted love child. Efforts to hide this struggle amounted to desperately pushing down a lid on an emotional volcano, ready to blow! It consumed me though I tried to feign a disposition of being in full control.

Oh how hard I tried to be good enough to make Him want me, yet despite my best efforts I failed miserably to get this deep sense of meaningful connection between us realized.

I wanted to be in the Cool Kids Club that God was the captain of but instead I felt like the ridiculed flunky because of all of the stuff going on in my life.

I trust that many holding this book and beginning to walk through these pages together with me, can relate to how despairing and hurtful this can feel.

The distress in my heart was so great and securing a meaningful connection with God seemed so elusive that I made attempts to cure myself by filling the emptiness of what my heart longed for from God with substitutes. Unfortunately, I wound up causing myself greater injury as I sought alternatives for intimacy with God that I could intellectually grasp and measure up to. Each alternative, or better said, substitute, for God's love that I gathered for myself, let me down hard and carelessly; unmercifully dashing me and my expectations to the ground; for nothing can compare with the *real* thing.

Heckled by the impotent struggle and shattered by the fruitless results, I finally mustered the courage. In an exhausted, pitiful whisper I asked God, "Why don't you want me?" My life surely *looked* like He didn't want me and the lack of meaningful connection and relational closeness made me *feel* like He didn't want me.

With that vulnerable question, I accepted His invitation to scoop up my wilted frame and calm my whimpering with His touch, His love, and His song:

> For the LORD your God is living among you. He is a mighty savior. He will take delight in you with gladness. With his

> love, he will calm all your fears. He will rejoice over you with joyful songs.
> Zephaniah 3:17 (NLT)

> "All that the Father giveth me shall come to me; and him that cometh to me I will in no wise cast out." (John 6:37, KJV).

Emptying myself before God and asking Him that question redirected the course of my life!

God had been offering me a piggy-back ride to escort and navigate me away from my fears, unbelief, and issues. I finally jumped aboard for the ride of a lifetime.

Journey to Love!

> For this cause I bow my knees unto the Father of our Lord Jesus Christ, Of whom the whole family in heaven and earth is named, That he would grant you, according to the riches of his glory, to be strengthened with might by his Spirit in the inner man; That Christ may dwell in your hearts by faith; that ye, being rooted and grounded in love, May be able to comprehend with all saints what is the breadth, and length, and depth, and height; And to know the love of Christ, which passeth knowledge, that ye might be filled with all the fullness of God.
> Ephesians 3:14-19 (KJV)

10 Years of *Journey To Love*

Dear Reader & Friends,

It is such a joy to be able to share this tenth anniversary edition of *Journey to Love* with you! Some of the content has been refined and a few points sharpened, but the essence of the original work remains.

I have received testimonies of the helpfulness of this book in the lives of people who are now experiencing greater freedom and intimacy in their relationship with the Lord.

This edition now includes a study guide. This guide, affectionately referred to as the *Journey Journal* was also written ten years ago, but only used during speaking engagements. It has proven to be a useful tool for group or personal study, now found right in the back of the printed and e-book versions.

The *Journey Journal* was designed to encourage you to do the hard work of peeling away the layers and unearthing the fears, unbelief, and ish-yous that may be preventing a progressively deepening relationship and meaningful connection with the Lord.

The study guide is so important to me because this book was intended for more than just storytelling. This book was purposed to help connect people with God by helping them see Him more clearly through my limitations and frailty that I so openly share about; the study guide helps draw out this purpose.

May you confidently approach God, look to Him in all of your ways, and enjoy His powerfully loving embrace that awaits you.

With love,

Janeen

Chapter One

Selective Hearing

"Now the word of the LORD came unto Jonah the son of Amittai, saying, Arise, go to Nineveh, that great city, and cry against it; for their wickedness is come up before me." Jonah 1:1-2 (KJV)

Jonah was one of my favorite Bible stories growing up. It was far more exciting than any cartoon I had ever seen! Imagine it for a moment: a prophet disobeys God, runs to hide from Him and then God catches him like a baseball, using the belly of a huge fish as His supernatural baseball glove. Wow!

As an adult, I've heard some question whether this book in the Bible is truth or fairy tale, but seeing as Jesus referred to it during his ministry (Matthew 12:38-42; 16:4; Luke 11:29-32), I'm all in of the belief that it is truth!

I wonder what else was inside of the belly of the fish with Jonah as he sat in there, isolated from the rest of the world, in that whale-sized holding tank. In the midst of the sounds, smells, and possibly other undigested critters furiously flapping about in terror, what was Jonah thinking about?

Distance from your loved ones and support system can be lonely and painful. Being granted leave, scheduling time off work, and booking the flight can solve it most of the time, in one form or another, but there is another level of pain that distance can cause that cuts far deeper.

Remember the pain-filled cry that Jesus let out from the cross, as He experienced distance with the Father?

> "And about the ninth hour Jesus cried with a loud voice, saying, Eli, Eli, lama sabachthani? that is to say, My God, my God, why hast thou forsaken me?" (Matthew 27:46, KJV).

The disconnection grinding deep into His soul was happening at that moment on the cross because the Father was turning His back on Jesus. God is holy and can't look upon sin and it was at that very moment that Jesus became the sacrifice and all of the world's sin was placed upon Him.

Jesus's anguish was not pain-filled because of mere distance in miles between His earthly location and the Father's heavenly location; it was relational distance.

I had no whale-sized holding tank to explain the distance that I felt and I surely was not bearing the sins of the world upon a cross, but I was experiencing distance in my relationship with God, like He was giving me the cold shoulder or the silent treatment and it hurt bad.

Where was God? My God? My Savior? My Maker?

Can You Hear Me

Jonah hailed from the town of Gath Hepher (2 Kings 14:25). This town was given as an allotment for Zebulun (Joshua 19:13) who was one of Jacob's sons, one of the twelve tribes of Israel. I wonder what this town's environment was like that helped nurture the young Jonah.

Zebulun's mother was Leah and she was the wife of Jacob but not the *only* wife and *definitely* not his favorite. Leah wound up married to Jacob because her dad tricked Jacob into marrying her. Though there are some cultural realities involved here which are very different from ours today, the thought of being in that situation just feels so humiliating and it makes me just want to give Leah a big hug.

To make matters worse, Jacob made clear that he did not want Leah but wanted Leah's sister Rachel; of whom her dad made the original deal for her marriage to Jacob too and of whom was Jacob's *favorite* wife. Ouch!

Leah was not loved but her situation mattered to God. He was especially kind to her and granted her a special grace: children.

> "When the LORD saw that Leah was not loved, he opened her womb, but Rachel was barren" (Genesis 29:31, NIV).

It is logical to conclude that Leah didn't believe that she mattered to Jacob and that she had unmet expectations in her relationship with him. Those reasonable expectations found in healthy relationships that communicate love include devoting time and attention, being intentional and protective toward maintaining intimate closeness, and guarding against anything that would come against your union. It hurts when these elements are not in place and distance and cold indifference are found instead. I believed I didn't matter to my husband or to God.

Speak Up A Little

"Hey," was the half-hearted greeting offered to me.

I was more hurt than angered by this greeting because I was still in the hospital after giving birth to our third child less than eight hours before.

"So, did they bring the papers down yet?" he asked, a bit sarcastically.

"Yes," I answered.

"What did you name her?" he insisted.

I responded somewhat sheepishly with a joke and with a name contrary to what he wanted. He cursed me bitterly for nearly half an hour and broke for a couple of minutes only when the nurse took my newborn to have her picture and an ink impression of her hands and feet taken.

He wasn't hearing my need for love at that extremely vulnerable moment. I needed him to protect me and be intimately near me.

For years it had been *my* responsibility to make things happy and calm—or so I believed. The success of our marriage and family life hinged on my ability to accommodate and cope with his extreme emotional instability—or so I thought.

The problem was that I was too often unable to tell where the emotional mines were hidden in the field of our relationship. I tip-toed around, one cautious step after another, to avoid setting off an explosion and I eventually grew tired.

I had been accustomed to measured communication and primarily used open-ended questioning. I had lost—or better said *abdicated*—my right to question him directly about anything. I didn't speak up. This indirect method of communication seemed to appease him and prevent volatile verbal outbursts. But this event in the hospital affected me in a way that no other negative exchange had before.

My baby daughter was so precious to me; so soft and tiny. *My* baby girl! The emotional trauma that resulted from this verbal assault as I lay there on the gurney made me feel as though I had been divested of the right to ever expect her to call me her *Mama*. Lying there silent against the abusive berating and hushed into a silent stupor, I was emotionally bankrupt and therefore too impoverished to raise her fitly.

As the barrage continued, I looked over at the forms I had completed earlier that morning, bearing the name he wanted for her. This time I was too weak to speak up in effort to appease the shaming, rageful assault by trying to reason with him. For once, the challenge to turn this negative into a positive defeated me. I didn't even have the strength to pick up the forms and show him. Self-talk and positive thinking failed, seemingly, for the first time. The task set before me on that gurney was just too great, well beyond my abilities. I was too weary to problem solve his overreaction to my sheepish joking around. So I rolled off the gurney and waddled to the bathroom with bitter hot tears streaming down my face as they so often did.

I wasn't just hurt from the emotional ripping but frustrated to tears because I could not reason with him to avoid this conflict and mistreatment. I was humiliated and ashamed that this was the man who was charged with covering and caring for me. *Wasn't he?*

I wondered if any of the people from our community who were dropping by the hospital to celebrate the new addition to the family overheard any of his cruel outburst. Is that what I had been unable to identify in their fixed stares at me? Did they know the shame of the truth behind our closed doors?

I began to shake uncontrollably. I was simply overwhelmed.

"Lord help me," is all I could whisper in my heart; my prayer.

Knowing that my two-year-old son and sixteen-month-old daughter would soon be there to meet their new baby sister, I mustered enough strength to pull myself together and not break down with the reviving help of a nice warm shower.

On this day of my infant's birth, the church we attended was the focus of a feature story on the front page of the Community section of the most widely distributed newspaper in our home state. Interviews for the article had been going on for about a year, and finally the story was in print with the picture of the man I was married to—the church's senior pastor—right there on the front page, just hours before my daughter was born.

As I stood in the shower, the warm water was on track to providing me with a few moments of the quiet time that I needed to get myself together—or so I hoped.

My labor and delivery nurse was in there with me too as an extra measure of precaution due to a slight challenge experienced with the pregnancy and delivery. Heartbreakingly, she added to the turmoil and further interrupted me from this moment of peace that I seriously needed.

She was of a different faith than I and commenced to interview me about the news article and what life was like as an "evangelical Christian," right there as I showered. Because the leaders in her faith community were required to take a vow of celibacy, she was far more interested in probing about what it was like for me being married to a senior pastor. She was also not careful in voicing her resentment at the thought of my husband being married to me and what a distraction it was to his purpose of serving God. *Mercy!*

Between my brief answers to the extremely inquisitive nurse, I put my head under the shower water to hide from the cruel ferociousness of my mental struggle. Looking back, during those moments, I am more aware than ever before that it was God alone who kept me from succumbing to mental madness.

As I tried to let the warm shower water's ministry take effect, my attempt at peace was suddenly interrupted again, but this time by an old Gospel song that popped up into my mind: "Your Grace And Mercy."

> "Your grace and mercy
> Have brought me through
> I'm living this moment
> Because of You
> I just want to thank you
> And praise you too
> Your grace and mercy
> Have brought me through."

The lyrics to that old gospel song by Franklin Williams kept wrapping around in my mind and they were grinding deep into my soul.

Now torrentially swirling in my mind, the song was reduced to one word: mercy. I could not reconcile that attribute of God to my life right then.

Where are you God? Why won't you answer me? Don't you see what I'm going through? Don't you care?

Where could I run and hide for cover? My stack was getting ready to blow! I just needed everybody and everything to *shut up* and *give me a minute*: I just had a baby!

I believed I had to keep it all together. The attention that I would have garnered from a meltdown just then would have cost too much! Or would it have? To who? To what?

My typical *shielded* response to such turmoil would be to appear unaffected and deliver a calm and gentle response, all the while gravely clinging to the desperate hope of appeasing and bringing the turmoil to an end. In other words, I would put on a façade, a mask. The problem now was that over the years I grew out of touch with my heart because it had become fused with the shield.

As I caught sight of myself in the bathroom mirror after my shower, I didn't recognize the woman staring back at me. It frightened me. I didn't know why or even how I got to this comatose state. I knew I was alive on the inside, but I had so internalized the constant messages hurled at me that told me I was useless, that vitality no longer shone through my eyes. I really looked like I had a mask on and it moved me enough to seek an answer.

There in that bathroom, for the first time in a long time, in the midst of all of the turmoil, I removed the shield and allowed myself to connect to the innermost part of me. The truest, deepest part: my heart.

How had one human being gained such power over me, and how on earth had I allowed my own standards with him and others to be brought down so low to nothing? Aren't I living righteously enough to deserve better? What's up with all of this?

I was ashamed and embarrassed that my relationship with God felt the same as my marital relationship: distant. He was a loving God and I was His child, so how could this be? The coldness, the indifference?

Well, it turns out that *I* wasn't being a very good listener to what God had been trying to say.

Ish-You

My mama had a way of inviting my siblings and I to listen to her. It was probably very similar in your family, too. God has a way, actually many ways, of inviting us to listen to Him. In the case with Jonah, it was pretty straightforward:

> "Now the word of the LORD came unto Jonah the son of Amittai, saying: Go to the great city of Nineveh and preach against it…" (Jonah 1:1-2a, KJV).

The words of my mama would come to us saying, "It's time for dinner." She wasn't providing us with an auditory skills test. What she said, though not a question, required a demonstrated response. It didn't matter if our game of hide and seek was tied and we just needed one more round to settle the score, when she said, "It's time for dinner," we'd better stop what we were doing and go inside and eat dinner. If not, there would be a larger issue created that would certainly be straightened out by way of spanking or other punishment.

Imagine how it must feel for the God of the universe to call *you* by name and then ask *you* to do something for Him. I remember how proud I used to feel when my mama would tell me to go and get my brother and sister and tell them that she said, "It's time to come home, now." Minus the cape, I felt like a superhero.

Even though it was pseudo choice, whether or not I would carry out her request of me (I had better or else), I was excited and proud to carry out the messenger task and speak on her behalf, because her name was proven and loaded with authority. I would get the warm fuzzies as I pulled out a bit of a deeper voice, declaring to my siblings, "Mama said…"

Called by name by God and commissioned to deliver a message in His name—how could that be an issue for anyone? Who would balk at that or even more brazenly, who would ignore a direct request and flatly not respond at all to Him?

Jonah clearly had an issue with God's request to deliver His message to the people of Nineveh. Jonah balked and brazenly ignored God. Well, actually, Jonah did listen to God but responded by intentionally heading in the opposite direction of where God requested that he go.

Well, I had an issue but I spell it and define it differently: *Ish-You*. It is part acronym and part pronoun and it stands for an *Imagined State/Status* that is *Hampering You* from a progressively deepening relationship with the Lord.

An issue occurs when the enemy has dressed up a lie to make it look like the truth and then cunningly engages you in a head game to get you to believe it. It's not just any old lie, no! It is a direct, deceptive misrepresentation of God's Word and God's voice. That's what happened to Eve in the Garden of Eden. The enemy antagonized her to doubt and not believe what God said about eating the forbidden fruit:

> Now the serpent was more crafty than any of the wild animals the LORD God had made. He said to the woman, "Did

God really say, 'You must not eat from
any tree in the garden'?"
Genesis 3:1 (NIV)

Note also that the enemy will minimize or misrepresent the promises of God and will certainly not remind us of the unsavory consequences for our disobedient, selective hearing.

The enemy is relentless and is always trying to disconnect us relationally from God.

Another example of how this strategy of the enemy manifests itself is in the case of the tied game of hide-and-seek. He will say something like, "Come on just one more round of hide-and-seek; we gotta break this tie. Mama understands and won't mind one bit."

You have a solid relationship with your mama and know very well that her track record is proven. When she says to come in and eat dinner now, that is an absolute directive. There is nothing confusing about what she said or grey area available to interpret it any other way.

Surely my mama loved me dearly but when I disobeyed, I wound up in time out. My relationship with her would certainly experience frustration as a result of my heeding to the deceptive lie of the enemy. Very important to note is that during my time out, our bond was never broken but our abiity to relate to one another was certainly hampered.

Jonah was a prophet and knew God's voice and Word solidly, but wound up in time out for three days and three nights in the belly of a huge fish.

There is *something* in us that is enticed by wandering down the lesser, godless path. We will explore that *something* in a later chapter but note that our decision is born out of our own heart's wayward desires. Eve wanted the fruit, we wanted to play another round of hide and seek, and Jonah didn't want to go to Nineveh. The desire for the lesser path was already in the heart.

> Let no man say when he is tempted, I am tempted of God: for God cannot be tempted with evil, neither tempteth he any man: But every man is tempted, when he is drawn away of his own lust, and enticed.
> James 1:13-14 (KJV)

We will examine Jonah's *ish-you* a bit later but for now, let me share with you about mine.

So what was my *ish-you*? My *ish-you* was that deep in my heart, I did not believe that God loved me or that He even cared about my life. The enemy had been whispering that lile to me my entire life and I was already predisposed to believe it.

My life surely *looked* like He didn't love me and the lack of meaningful connection and relational closeness made me *feel* like He didn't care about me.

It was definitely a lie of the enemy that God didn't love me or care, and I embraced that lie, hook, line, and sinker and as a result, became horribly tangled up and ensnared. This broad net of a lie snatches up a lot of good folk.

Do you recognize the strength of each tightly woven knot?

"*Big* God doesn't care about *little* me."

"Obey God without fail (every do not, shall not and will not), no questions asked."

"You don't measure up, but if you are good enough and finally get your act together, you will gradually leave the naughty list."

"You should know better than to bother God with your foolish, finite problems."

"God is far too busy doing God stuff and He is not to be trifled with."

This unrelenting, demonic whispering, intending to hypnotize God's beloved children into an insecure stupor, is the mindset that the enemy aims to inflict and infect us with. The enemy desires to create a breeding ground in our minds of doubt, discouragement, and defeat to influence us in such a way as to create space and distance between us and our Maker, hampering our relationship.

God was trying to get my attention because there were some things that He wanted me to hear and to say.

> "For I know the thoughts that I think toward you, saith the Lord, thoughts of peace, and not of evil, to give you an expected end" Jeremiah 29:11, KJV).

But until He *fixed* my marriage, I wasn't hearing *anything* He was trying to say to me, not realizing that my marriage was not the root cause of what I believed to be my issue.

__Journaling__

God told Jonah to go and deliver a message for Him to the city of Nineveh, which was the capital city of the ancient Assyrian empire. Assyria was founded by Ashur, Noah's grandson (Genesis 10:11-12, KJV). Yes, *that* Noah, the righteous man:

> "This is the account of Noah and his family. Noah was a righteous man, blameless among the people of his time, and he walked with God" (Genesis 6:9, NIV).

Do you remember the story about the ark and how Noah built it though it had never rained on the earth before? People laughed and heckled him, but he believed God and kept on until the task of building the ark was complete; a sea-worthy structure that took many, many years to construct.

Noah faithfully stood on his faith in God, despite the nay-saying, wicked climate that was all around him. He believed God!

> "Go to the great city of Nineveh and preach against it, because its wickedness has come up before me" (Jonah 1:2, NIV).

So what happened? How did Nineveh, the capital city of Assyria, the land founded by Ashur, Noah's grandson, wind up being a wicked place? How did we get from *"walking faithfully with God"* to *"their wickedness is come up before me"*?

It is quite a thought to think that Ashur was not influenced by his grandad and did not share any allegiance to his God, the *true* God.

Nonetheless, I could find no record to help answer what was the root cause for the apparent spiritual demise; it was not immediately visible to the eye. Similar was the case with my marriage. How did it get like this? What was the answer for its awful condition?

The turmoil in my marriage was so boisterous, obnoxious, and intrusive that that's what had my full attention and what I identified as the root cause of my issue. The real root cause did not come into full view until I settled into a few moments of peace and quiet while journaling.

When I was pregnant, someone gave me a journal as a baby shower gift and that's when the practice began for me.

Other than the grace of God, I don't know what provoked my first entry. It was so cryptic. I had such a fear that my journal would be discovered and read, that I resorted to these Pig-Latin type entries. Looking back, I have no idea what kind of language or code system that I was using.

Over time, I began to emote honestly in my journal. I'd actually written through the whole thing but was compelled to continue. I looked forward to the honest, internal dialogue.

Within a year or two of beginning the discipline of journaling, I decided to organize all of my entries. Since I'd written through the entire baby shower journaling gift, I now had entries amassed on scraps of paper stashed in coat pockets, old purses, hat boxes, in the margins of books, not to mention a mound of church bulletins. Trying to organize all of those entries was a thinly-veiled way for me to unearth the root cause of my ish-you and ready my heart and mind for the big reveal: the root cause of my ish-you was me not being a very good listener to what God had been saying to me.

Loner-Ville

Was Jonah a *loner*?

Other than God, this Bible story does not make mention of him sharing his life with anyone, personally. As wildly exciting as this story is, how is it that there is not one conversation recorded between him and a friend, cousin, mentor, or sibling?

God did not intend for us to live isolated or alone.

> Two are better than one because they have a good return for their labor: If either of them falls down, one can help the other up. But pity anyone who falls and has no one to help them up. Also, if two lie down together, they will keep warm. But how can one keep warm alone? Though one may be overpowered, two can defend themselves. A cord of three strands is not quickly broken.
> Ecclesiastes 4:9-12 (NIV)

I was a loner for many reasons and I allowed this toxic marriage to drive me further into isolation.

My first weeks at home with my infant, I remember being extremely hungry and sleep-deprived as the baby was not yet sleeping through the night and my other two children were still in diapers.

One day, late in the morning, I was at the kitchen sink bathing and washing my tiny infant's hair. I was ignoring the doctor's instructions to stay off my feet so that I could heal and recover properly. I had no choice because no other help was allowed in our home, at that time.

Anyway, as I was giving her a bath and beginning to wash her hair, the phone rang and woke up my other two toddlers. I didn't answer the phone because I had just gotten a little gentle baby wash in her eye and needed to tend to that while calming the other two, now clinging to my knees.

The phone kept ringing! Usually around the fourth or fifth ring people assume no one is there and hang up…but it kept ringing! Suddenly, I got a stabbing pain in my back, as though I were going into labor all over again. As I winced in pain, I heard the sound of a closing car door in the driveway at the church next door—we lived in the church's parsonage. Due to the constant chaos of our house, this sound typically triggered a great degree of anxiety. I did dread visitors stopping by that I wasn't prepared to receive. I wasn't presentably dressed, to say the least, and definitely not looking very preacher's wife-like.

There was only a little sheer curtain at the back window and people could see in, if they made an effort. They would put their face close enough to the window and though it typically made me giggle to see the fog created by the hot breath of the *curious*, I was definitely not laughing now. I started to stress out and panic in a way like I never had before.

At the sound of the front yard gate opening, my two toddlers scooted into one of the back rooms, and I grabbed the soapy bubbly baby and whisked her upstairs but not before soaking the floor with my blood!

As I gently called down to my toddlers to go watch TV in the living room (far away from the sight on the kitchen floor), I was crying so hard from the stress of those frantic moments, that it certainly prolonged the healing of my frail body. I was a physical wreck!

Though there were times when he would lead me to believe that I could get some rest or walk outside for a few minutes to get a break, I really couldn't. It just never seemed to quite work out. I would hear the children wail within minutes, if not seconds, of my departure and I'd immediately stop whatever I was doing and jump back to check things out.

Upon returning in and inspecting the children in the play room, where he was supposed to be watching and caring for them, he'd angrily grumble at me, "Janeen, why do you always second guess what I am doing or feel the need to intervene. Fine then, you take care of it all!"

Too often they were crying because he had not checked the temperature of the bottle before giving it to them straight from the microwave—too hot! They would be placed on their backs to nurse the bottle without help.

If I took a nap for a break, the *ready* beep of the microwave woke me straight up and made me jump and run. About two years after the bottle phase ended in our home, the beep of the microwave still unsettled me.

I wasted my time with trying to prepare for my break. I would feed them and change their diapers and request my break to coincide with their rigid nap schedule. But inevitably, if the children were asleep and he wanted to play, he would dismiss my plea and dissertation for the need to maintain their schedule. I would be in agony dealing with his decision to wake them and throw them off schedule AGAIN!

It wasn't only that he would give them hot bottles but he was a gun owner, too. He had many guns and at this time did not own a gun cabinet. He stored them in creative locations all over the house which I would find, to my horror, while doing chores. Food debris and dishes to include steak knives and silverware were regularly on the floors around the area where he reclined during his *watch*.

C'mon, man! We've got crawling toddling toddlers in here!

The children may have been crying for a lot of reasons. I jumped and stopped whatever *break* activity I was doing every time I heard them cry. And more often than not, every time I jumped to attend to them, they and I were thankful that I did.

One day, I awakened with the left side of my facial muscles sagging just a smidgen lower than the facial muscles on my right side. My body was telling me (in more ways than one) that it had had enough!

Why didn't I ask the older, wiser deacons' wives to pray for me? Join a mom's group? Borrow a stroller and get some fresh air? Have a teen from the church come and sit for an hour so I could nap or ask their mothers to help me out with a meal? That's right, there are no neighbors in Loner-Ville and yet there are tons of these towns, with the same name, same population count (one), throughout the world. Fascinating!

One of the main reasons for my decision to live life as a loner was because I had erroneously expected and understood that God's love meant insulation from hurt, hardness, and the storms of life, but this was not the case. I was subconsciously making an effort to affirm this ideal in my loner way. If you're not around others, they can't hurt you. But how do you protect yourself from yourself? Self-harm is a contributor towards some of the ills that we face too.

Living life is a contact sport, of sorts. I wrongfully believed that God's love equaled divine insulation. In part, what I thought was relational disconnection and cold indifference between God and I was actually His unwelcomed invitation to train me to confidently engage life in this fallen world. For one, He gave me a voice and I needed to speak up and use it. I had to learn how to balance my weight and throw a good punch, to be prepared for the storms that this sin-stained world had in store.

God was actually engaging me, calling to me to train me but I had selective hearing. I had no need to feel disappointed by God or frustrated or dejected. The Christian life is not lived insulated from the ills of this world. We must box and we must go the distance. Also, boxers must spar to learn and become good fighters. God was trying to teach me.

> "Everyone who competes in the games goes into strict training. They do it to get a crown that will not last; but we do it to get a crown that will last forever" (1 Corinthians 9:25, NIV).

My prayer for us, as we look back over our life, before we depart for our eternal home is to be able to echo the same as the Apostle Paul:

> "I have fought a good fight, I have finished my course, I have kept the faith" (2 Timothy 4:7, KJV).

Don't doubt God. Don't lose faith in His Word and all that He has promised.

God stopping every storm headed our way would cause our muscles to atrophy. We must be able to take a lick and keep on ticking but that only comes from development, from walking through the storms of life, *with God.*

God cares about His children and will use any and everything to draw us close to Him; close to Him is the safest place for us to be. We must choose to accept His invitation for a piggyback ride away from our fears and unbelief to grow stronger muscles and to grow into a deeper, personal knowledge of His love for us. We don't belong in Loner-Ville.

> "Oil and perfume make the heart glad, and the sweetness of a friend comes from his earnest counsel" (Proverbs 27:9, ESV).

My disorientation, resulting from my erroneous expectations of divine insulation drove me to build that shield around my heart. My shield was double-sided in its purpose. It was supposed to protect me from the pain of unmet expectations that I had of people and of God.

I believed that lie that says God insulates those He loves. But in this life we will experience things that hurt us and that we don't like.

> "...for he maketh his sun to rise on the evil and on the good, and sendeth rain on the just and on the unjust" (Matthew 5:45, KJV).

I internalized my feelings of shame, neglect, and embarrassment due to what I believed was my second-class status with God.

I was going to insulate myself in His seeming absence. This thinking and behavior contributed to the feeling of distance between God and me. Even worse was that I had grieved the Spirit of God, living in my heart. The Spirit of God comforts, guides, and teaches. I couldn't hear Him well enough through that shield. Wallowing in my ish-you in Loner-Ville is what I continued to do.

Lights, Camera, Action

> "Do not make friends with a hot-tempered man, do not associate with one easily angered, or you may learn their ways and get yourself ensnared" (Proverbs 22:24-25, NIV).

Fast forward about two years. It was our oldest child's first school play. It was such a precious occasion. The camera and wardrobe were all prepared the night before—such high hopes for this moment in the life of our family. We had to have him there at the school several minutes early to rehearse and prepare for his thespian debut.

My youngest child was up early and needed a bath. I woke up the two older children and got them fed and dressed, as usual. I then cared for my own needs by hurriedly rinsing what needed to be soaked and powdering what needed to be painted. All this was done to ensure that our little thespian got to the school on time. I ran upstairs to find *him* still in the bed. We needed to be walking out of the door in fewer than ten minutes even to be *on time* because by now, we were too late to be there early. *How could he?* I wondered. *Where's the consideration?*

"Honey, you need to get up," I told him, on behalf of our little thespian. "We're going to be late, and I was hoping we'd get good seats so that he can see us watching him from the audience."

"Janeen! I'm coming!" he carelessly responded.

As he finally rolled out of the bed, I began to take the curlers out of my hair. Last thing for me to do, though I'd planned to do this in the car on the way!

The children were now ready and waiting at the bottom of the stairs. I gathered my brush and comb to finish styling my hair in the car when to my surprise I heard the shower turn on. He was climbing into the shower! I was outraged!

I knocked on the bathroom door and reminded him how late we were…to no avail! I returned to my vanity, feeling as if I were in shackles with the sound of the ticking clock sickening me. He came out of the bathroom before taking his shower and wanted to know why I was making such a big fuss. I remained focused on my purpose. I just hadn't time to spare for an argument.

I suggested that he give me the keys to one of *his* four cars in our driveway so I could drive the children to the school. I promised to save a seat for him, which didn't help. He was adamant in his rejection. He accused I was trying to embarrass him by attending the event without him.

Again, I tried to keep the conversation focused on the urgent issue—getting our little thespian to the school on time. That was the priority at hand but was quickly slipping away and was also clearly not a priority we shared. He then responded by grumbling in an almost unintelligible gibberish, similar to that of a stammering drunk.

By now, the children had left from the bottom of the stairs and turned on cartoons in the family room; our little thespian was now running late. I was livid! I was hurting for our little one, too. I returned to my vanity and dressing area feeling woeful. He had entered and exited the bathroom again and again, and now we were both screaming at the top of our lungs. I was so angry at feeling caged because the consequence was being felt by our little thespian.

In our house, it was rare that my voice matched the same level and intensity as his but the mama bear naturally runs to protect her cubs, even if it is directly into the path of harm's way.

"You are a controlling b—," he screamed at me, and I fired back: "You are a sorry man, you punk." With that, he walked right over to my vanity and dared me to say it again. And I did. At which he repeated "B—" and I countered with "Punk," back and forth we exchanged about five times nearly nose to nose and then, *SLAP!* He struck me across the face! I hit him back several times; I probably looked like a wild windmill.

It was dangerous.

My shield was not doing a very good job of protecting me. Where was God?

This arguing, fussing and misery could not continue. More tears and promises for three more years until one day I *finally* listened, well I listened a *little* bit. God was faithfully asking me to hop on for that piggyback ride away from my fears and unbelief and ish-you-so, I *finally* took a baby step toward Him.

The Deck on that "Holy-Day"

It was the holiday season and his mama passed away. We flew home to California to bury her and enjoy as best we could the rest of the holidays with our families. As the time drew near for us to return home to New England, he informed me that he would not be returning with the children and me. Mind you, the children and I had flown without him to California for the funeral, too. (Those of you who have traveled with children on an airplane from one coast to another can surely appreciate my buckled knees at the thought of having to do this again alone).

We made it to the airport with little money. We had just enough to eat at the fast-food restaurant in the airport as we waited to board our return flight. A deacon from the church would be awaiting our arrival to carry us home from the airport.

Often when we returned from our winter holiday vacation, our basement would be flooded and there would be no heat and no food but this trip, I was prepared! I had serviced and cleaned the portable kerosene heaters, cleaned the sump pump in the basement, and stocked the freezer and cupboards with food. We were ready!

As the children and I landed back to our New England home, to my surprise another member of the church greeted us at the airport to take us home. My husband bitterly despised this member of our church family because *he* said that he and his family were too *nosy*.

This member and his family were genuinely concerned for the children and me. A cold front had hovered over New England days before our arrival and with the hour being so late, it was doubtful that the home's temperature would be habitable. I tried to brush off his concern by highlighting the good on our holiday vacation, especially the food. I was also working overtime to explain how prepared we were for whatever cold and dark conditions that might lay on the other side of our doorway.

As we pulled up to the house, it did seem abnormally dark. Not just the kind of darkness no electricity brings…it was like the kind of darkness portrayed in horror movies (the only thing missing was a bunch of vultures circling).

It was about 2:00 a.m. and the children and I were bushed. The church member waited in the kitchen and remarked on how bitterly cold it was in the parsonage we called home. I quickly began a check of the premises, looking forward to giving him the all-clear signal. I assured him that I was prepared for the cold this time and had cleaned the kerosene heaters, etc., but as I flipped the switch on the heaters, nothing happened. I also began to notice a weird, unfamiliar odor in the house.

He helped to try and start the heaters as the children were celebrating their homecoming in the back bedrooms. I assured him that we would be just fine. I would turn on the stove and fashion a bed sheet over the kitchen doorway to keep in the heat for warmth and we'd hang out in the kitchen until the house warmed a bit (it was a familiar process for me). He strongly objected because it was near zero in the house and it would take a *long* time to get heat to the children's back bedrooms. Also, he said, he and his wife had made provision for us in the event we needed to stay with them because as he put it, they just had a *feeling* that something like this might happen. He said that he just couldn't stomach leaving us in the house in that condition.

I tried to smile and convince him otherwise and assure him that we would be okay. He conceded, but only on the condition I would promise to call his family if it was too much to bear. I agreed. He reluctantly left, and I called California to let the family know that we had arrived back to our New England home safely.

On the phone, I mentioned to my sister that there was a strange odor in the house and now to add were some odd scratching noises I had just begun to hear. My sister asked where the noises were coming from and promised to hold the line as I went to investigate further.

I thought that it might be the dogs, seeing as their cage was near the window by the phone but they had never been able to reach from their cages all the way over to the windows before. I opened the basement door to discover that it was severely flooded with more than two feet of water; I was disgusted! I then followed the scratching noises which were now coming from behind our big screen television: *Rats!* I was horrified!

They were in the walls throughout the house. I thought I would die. I couldn't stand there in disbelief too long though because of the children! They were still celebrating in the back rooms. I ran back there frantic, seeing now the shredded pieces of fabric throughout the carpet flooring, produced by the nesting rodents. I quickly composed myself enough to feign a smiley-face mask and tell the children that the kitchen was now warm from the stove heat and that it would be best to huddle in there for a while.

I returned to the phone and shared with my sister all I had discovered. She *clicked* over for me on her three-way phone line and dialed *him*. As I began to tell *him* the condition of the house, *his* response was, "What do you want me to do about it?" I desperately blurted out, "Well, when are you coming home?" His sharp response was: "I don't know."

"We need help," I squeaked out. "What am I supposed to do?"

"Janeen, I guess you'll just have to figure something out."

At that moment an irreversible shift happened in our relationship that changed things between him and me forever.

I had no money and no other resources to secure the help we needed. I hung up with my sister and turned to the perky faces of my three grinning babies whose cheeks and noses were now red. In desperation, I closed my eyes, hugged them tight, and we jumped overboard into the crashing waves below. It was time to share my life, time to speak up, and time to use the voice God gave me.

That proverbial "jump" was my peeking out from behind my shield; it was not doing a good job at protecting me anyway as well that was no place to live nor was it what God intended for me. The turmoil and chaos was enough to drive me to open up and share about what was going on in my life. I packed my bags and left Loner-Ville, which was one of the things God had been trying to tell me to do. I was without resources to do anything about my situation and I was tired of it. So, I gave a few trusted people a front row glance of my life and as soon as I ended the phone call with my sister, I reached out to the church member and asked him and his family for help.

Transparency is transformative beyond my ability to describe in words. Lesson learned was though I thought I was divested of the right and conditioned to believe that I had no right, I was never without the ability to make personal life choices.

Actually, I had been choosing all along; silence is a choice.

Chapter Two

Tag! You're It!

> *"But Jonah rose up to flee unto Tarshish from the presence of the LORD, and went down to Joppa; and he found a ship going to Tarshish: so he paid the fare thereof, and went down into it, to go with them unto Tarshish from the presence of the LORD."*
> *Jonah 1:3 (KJV)*

The Place

It is amazing how at times we finite humans can think that we know better than God. God created the universe and He existed before time began. God knows the very number of strands of hair on our head and yet when He calls out to us to join Him in His work upon the earth, we scoff, questioning His wisdom when His request does not align with our expectations.

Why run and hide from God's call? It really is finite thinking to do such a thing. He's only inviting us along for a piggyback ride. Why not just climb aboard? One would have to overlook three major things about God to believe that running and hiding is a good choice to make in response to His request for us to do something for Him. For starters, our God is omnipresent; He is everywhere at the same time, making any excuse or reason we give a poor one. We can't go any place that God is not and where He is not in full control.

Some people have accused Jonah of being ridiculous for attempting to run away and hide from the omnipresent, omniscient, and omnipotent God.

Yes, he was being ridiculous, but not entirely. Based on his own understanding of God, Jonah had some basis to believe that he was making an intelligent decision.

In Jonah's time of on earth, God was local. He had an address. He was present in a temple in the holy of holies between the cherubims on the ark of the covenant.

> And there I will meet with thee, and I will commune with thee from above the mercy seat, from between the two cherubims which are upon the ark of the testimony, of all things which I will give thee in commandment unto the children of Israel.
>
> Exodus 25:22 (KJV)

> O Lord of hosts, God of Israel, that dwellest between the cherubims, thou art the God, even thou alone, of all the kingdoms of the earth: thou hast made heaven and earth.
>
> Isaiah 37:16 (KJV)

His people faithfully travelled to meet Him there, in Jerusalem, at least once a year and His presence was there at that place. This locale of their worship system was critically important and served as reminder that the Lord was one God, the only true God and different from the other gods served by other nations. Our God is incomparable.

The nations around them, including the entire Assyrian empire of which the Ninevites were a part of, were all polytheistic, serving many gods made with human hands and carved from sticks, stones, etc. These gods were transportable like stuffed animals or super-sized action figures.

Yahweh, God, was distinguishable from all other nations by *His* Oneness and also by being the children of Israel's *only* God. He was famously known for His presence being in *one* place so much so, that when war would come, the Israelites would take the ark (God's house) with them into battle, to represent the power that they had on their side. Conversely, their enemies would attempt to steal the house (the ark) as a spoil of war to mock the power or attempt to secure and harness God's power for themselves. The oneness of God was and still is a critical foundational understanding of who He is.

> One of the teachers of the law came and heard them debating. Noticing that Jesus had given them a good answer, he asked him, 'Of all the commandments, which is the most important?' 'The most important one,' answered Jesus, is this: 'Hear, O Israel: The Lord our God, the Lord is one. Love the Lord your God with all your heart and with all your soul and with all your mind and with all your strength.' The second is this: 'Love your

> neighbor as yourself.' There is no commandment greater than these.
> Mark 12:28-31 (NIV)

In this passage in Mark, Jesus was quoting that ancient text: "Hear, O Israel: The Lord our God, the Lord is one" (Deuteronomy 6:4, NIV).

God did dwell at that place, the ark, but He was not *exclusively* contained there. He is not limited or restricted by a place or time, as Jonah may have thought.

To further illustrate how deeply held this understanding of the locale was by both God's people and neighboring nations alike, we have the story of Naaman, a Syrian commander.

Naaman heard about the miracle-working God of the children of Israel. Naaman had leprosy and so traveled there to seek out the prophet of their God, in hopes of receiving a miracle for himself: getting his leprosy healed. God showed Naaman favor and granted him healing through His prophet Elisha. Naaman returned back to Syria, but not before taking several bags of dirt with him.

Based on his locale understanding of that time, taking some of the dirt was the equivalent of him taking the God of that land back with Him to Syria.

> Naaman said, 'If not, please let your servant at least be given two mules' load of earth; for your servant will no longer offer burnt offering nor will he sacrifice to other gods, but to the LORD.
> 2 Kings 5:17 (NASB)

Our human understanding is finite and today we can still tend to relegate God exclusively to one place disregarding His incomprehensible vastness, His omnipresence.

Whenever we choose to run and hide, we're essentially telling God that He is short-sighted and doesn't have all of the available facts and that we do. We are essentially telling God, by our waywardness, that we're smarter than He is and can make a better decision than what He has proposed for our lives.

Respond yes to His request of you. Doing so places you on board for a piggyback ride away from your fears, unbelief, and ish-yous.

There is a level of wisdom beyond what we can see and there is a peace and an inner confidence that we enable when we acknowledge the incomprehensible omnipresence of God. My childhood experiences of playing hide-and-seek was a good schoolmaster in the lesson of finite thinking and the value of embracing a level of knowing which far exceeded my own.

So, why run and hide from the call of God? In addition to God being everywhere at the same time, He is also omniscient. He knows all!

> "Where can I go from your Spirit? Where can I flee from your presence? If I go up to the heavens, you are there; if I make my bed in the depths, you are there" (Psalm 139:7-9, NIV).

Hide And Seek

Jonah would not have been my first choice as a teammate for a game of hide and seek. Hilarious now but very serious back then because as the first-grade champ, I had a reputation to protect! As the champ, there was something I could never quite figure out: I could never beat my parents at the game.

As hard I tried, I could not understand how it was that they could always find me, no matter how well I thought I hid. I mean, I was the champion in my class at school but how was it that my parents could win game after game after game! Of course now as an adult with children of my own, I understand quite well how they could find me. They were grown-ups and knew more than me.

I am confident that they decided to let me stay hidden after they'd actually found me.

"I wonder where she is hiding," they'd gently say, not giving up my hiding place too quickly, to make the game more fun and suspenseful for me. I did the same with my kids.

Our little house only had a couple of places that I could hide, but I didn't realize that as a hiding novice. My giggling, heavy breathing or toes sticking out from the corner of the sofa, were also dead giveaways. I would unintentionally make direct eye contact with them when peeking, but then thinking that my return behind the wall was so quick, that like a flash it caused them to not really see me but believe it was an apparition instead.

As a child, I did not realize or understand decision making like a grown up would; I couldn't see the fuller picture or evaluate all of the available options because I didn't know them all. My knowledge paled in comparison to theirs. Jonah foolishly thought he could run and hide from God but it was no different from me thinking God didn't see me in all that I was going through. God knows everything and we can't escape His gaze.

I got frustrated and didn't want to play hide and seek with my parents anymore because I couldn't win. Until I accepted and acknowledged that they were smarter than me, it was no fun at all!

In her wisdom at noticing my discouragement and frustration, the next round of the game, my mama came up behind me and whispered "Boo," grabbed me into her arms and tickled me. I enjoyed the closeness far more than what I could imagine at the joy of winning. I accepted and acknowledged that my mama knew more than me and playing hide and seek with them became fun. I wanted to play over and over again, even barely hiding just to be found in her embrace laughing to tears together.

Interestingly, when I would play the same game with my siblings in that same house, I would always win when I would hide in one special place. They'd *never* find me or even dare to look in my parents' closet. We were forbidden from playing in their room let alone freely rummaging through their closet, tucking behind their neatly hung clothes and sloppily rearranging their even rows of shoes. Unbeknownst to me, my father kept a shotgun in that closet. I did not know that was one of the major reasons they forbid us from playing in there.

Nonetheless, this one place was such a gold mine at keeping me hidden that on occasion they'd give up looking for me and I could emerge and dash out to the base, *safe*! This one particular time I remember falling asleep in their closet waiting for my siblings to find me. Well, it so happened that my mama found me and it was not a meeting of giggles and fun.

Just because my choice to hide in my parents' closet made sense as far as strategy to win goes, I knew better than to make the choice that I made because we all understood the *boundaries*. I'd crossed the line with this choice as my hiding place.

My parents didn't owe me an explanation for reason why hiding in their closet was off limits; I only needed to obey what they instructed me to do. Jonah needed to go to Nineveh and deliver God's message and I needed to hop on board for a piggyback ride. God's requests and rules are always for our good and His glory.

All in all, I believe I can speak for all of us and say that we are grateful God never hides from us, no matter what places we find ourselves in:

Clearly, we have lost sight of the incomprehensible vastness of God when we choose to run and hide from His call to us. He sees all, knows all and is all-powerful, regardless of our response.

> "If I rise on the wings of the dawn, if I settle on the far side of the sea, even there your hand will guide me, your right hand will hold me fast" (Psalm 139:9-10, NIV).

So why do we do it? Why do we run and hide from God's call to us to hop on for that piggyback ride? Internal conflict is one reason.

I Don't Believe It!

Would you believe it if someone punched you in the face and God told you to go hug and kiss them and tell them, "God loves you"? Though God did not tell Jonah to go hug and kiss the Ninevites after they punched him in the face,

I'd imagine extending God's mercy face-to-face with your enemy can feel pretty much the same as well as create an internal conflict and struggle to positively respond to God's request to do so.

According to the historian Josephus, Jonah was afraid to respond to God's request to go to Nineveh.

Stephen M. Miller, in his book, *The Complete Guide to the Bible*, puts it this way:

> Ordering a Jew to go to Nineveh and deliver a death threat would have made as much sense as sending a rabbi to Berlin in the early 1940's to tell Hitler he's in big trouble.
> The Complete Guide to the Bible

In my sanctified imagination, I can almost hear Jonah gasp, "I don't believe *this*," as his immediate response to God's request of him to go to Nineveh.

During this time, the capital city of the Assyrian empire was Nineveh. The Assyrians are credited with being a ruthlessly savage people of war, driven by their homage to their god, Assur. They believed Assur was supreme above all of their many other gods and to establish his preeminence required that they take over and lay claim all over the world in his name. It was their sacred commission; warfare was their cultural norm and regarded as divine service.

Aside from their mastery of siege warfare, inventors of iron weapons, expertise in horse and chariots, they would skin their enemies alive, impale them and commit other unmerciful, torturous acts, Stephen M. Miller continues:

The Assyrians are perhaps the most vicious empire this world has ever seen. Their idea of art suitable for framing and hanging on their palace walls includes stone chiseled images of dead Jews impaled on poles, as thick as fence posts...

Also etched in stone is an Assyrian king's brag after capturing a city in the 800s BC: 'Their men, young and old, I took as prisoners. Of some I cut off the feet and hands, of others I cut off the noses, ears, and lips. Of the young men's ears I made a mound. Of the old men's heads I built a minaret tower.'

Rebels got no respect from the Assyrians. Instead they got themselves dead in creative ways. One style of execution that Assyrian soldiers enjoyed was to slice open a captive's abdomen and stuff a wild cat inside, quickly sew up the abdomen, and then back away, watching the animal claw itself out. Terror, the Assyrians figured, was a great inhibitor. So they used it to keep enemies in their place—serving Assyria.

The Assyrians' fierce relentlessness to their cause finally won out where Jonah's homeland of Israel was concerned. They destroyed it, conquering it for themselves and their god!

So, regarding his divinely appointed request to go to Nineveh, they would say today, "Jonah wasn't *feeling* it" and he ran and hid from God's call. Was God not powerful enough to protect Jonah?

> If I say, 'Surely the darkness will hide me
> and the light become night around me,
> even the darkness will not be dark to you;
> the night will shine like the day, for darkness is as light to you.
> Psalm 139:11-12 (NIV)

The moment that Jonah decided to run and hide, Jonah took matters into his own hands and owned the results for the outcome of his decision. His entire world became skewed from center. His decision making and behavior got off track.

Let's face it, we tend to run and hide from God. We see it from the first days of mankind, as exemplified with Adam and Eve in the Garden of Eden (Genesis 3:7-10).

Scaredy-Cat or Wild-Cat

As I surveyed my own heart, and began growing a measure of courage to consider that the root cause of my problem was not my marital turmoil but rather that it was my selective hearing, I wondered if the root cause for Jonah's internal conflict and struggle, which influenced his decision to run and hide from God's call, was solely fear. Maybe he wasn't just some frightened victim after all.

This biblical account actually does not ascribe fear of the Ninevites or Assyria as being the reason at all for his response to run and hide from God's call. And, looking more closely, his behavior was very off and in my estimation, inconsistent with someone who is afraid.

> All the sailors were afraid and each cried out to his own god. And they threw the cargo into the sea to lighten the ship. But Jonah had gone below deck, where he lay down and fell into a deep sleep. The captain went to him and said, "How can you sleep? Get up and call on your god! Maybe he will take notice of us so that we will not perish.
>
> Jonah 1:5-6 (NIV)

The Bible describes that the storm on the sea was so violent that it nearly broke the ship into two pieces and yet Jonah was *fast* asleep during all of the ruckus. The sailors had to wake him up and ask him to pray to his god in hopes that the ritual would appease the fury unleashed against them by the supernatural. They'd hoped they could appease the gods enough to retreat from killing them, not knowing who Jonah's *God* was.

At that moment, the sailors didn't know that Jonah's God was the Omnipotent One that threw wind at the sea with ease, like a child skipping a rock across a pond, which produced the violent storm that they found themselves in. Up to that moment in the story of Jonah, there is no record that Jonah responded to them or prayed on the ship at all. I mean what's up with this behavior? Jonah was a prophet of the true and living God! Here the sailors are in fear for their life, throwing cargo overboard, and Jonah appears to be just *chilling* out in the midst of this unfolding life-threatening drama.

Up to this point of the story, Jonah himself claims that he fears the God of the heavens, "Who has made the sea and the dry land (Jonah 1:9)" and yet there is no record of him calling on God *at all* in prayer for help on the ship, in midst of this fierce storm! Yet Jonah actively hides from this same God because *He* requested that he go to Nineveh! Skeptical now toward believing that fear of the Ninevites had anything to do with his behavior because the degree of Jonah's responses just don't match the same degree of the circumstances that he was facing.

Well wouldn't you know it, the authority on the matter, the Bible, does reveal a different side of Jonah. The Interlinear Version of the Bible, in Jonah 4:1, revealed selfish anger and jealousy were in Jonah's heart. Dr. Paul H. Wright in his book, *Rose Then and Now Bible Map Atlas With Biblical Background and Culture*, offers a few other thoughts on Jonah's response, which had absolutely nothing to do with any fear of the Ninevites or the reputation of its ruthless Assyrian empire:

> Jonah son of Amittai of Gath-hepher, apparently a prophet of Jeroboam's royal court, was less concerned about individual human rights than the glory of his monarch's kingdom. While Amos and Hosea decried the social rot that stemmed from Jeroboam's policies, Jonah spoke of territorial expansion, encouraging Jeroboam's conquests...
>
> Jonah had a personal stake in the matter, for his own home town, Gath-hepher, on the northeastern shoulder of the high limestone ridge that separates Galilee from the Jezreel Valley, lay directly in Assyria's line of attack. If Israel could hang on to its Aramean vassals in the north, one of another of these states

could act as a buffer the next time Assyria burst on the scene...

To walk to Nineveh was dangerous enough, but should Jonah go, both his people and his own conscience would label him a traitor for warning their enemy of God's displeasures. On the other hand, should he refuse the call and Nineveh fall under divine judgement, Israel would finally be rid of the Assyrian threat and, with a clear eastern horizon, the nation could bask in the political and economic revival of Jeroboam II.

Additionally, as a prophet, every single prophecy declared must come true or you were dismissed as being a *false* prophet (Deuteronomy 18:21-22). Jonah knew that God was a merciful God. Decreeing judgment upon the Ninevites and then giving them forty days to think about it was risky. How were they going to spend their forty days? What if they repented and their foretold destruction didn't come to pass that he prophesied, at the end of those forty days? What would happen to Jonah's social status and career? The plot thickens.

> "If that nation against which I have spoken turns from its evil, I will relent concerning the calamity I planned to bring on it" (Jeremiah 18:8, NASB).

Though this passage was recorded after Jonah's time, the heart of God has been the same throughout time and will continue through eternity. God does not desire that anyone perish (2 Peter 3:9).

In addition to internal conflict and struggle, we also run and hide in response to outside or external influences, like being in the middle of our tie-breaking game of hide and seek and a funnel cloud appears and the tornado siren sounds—run and hide!

Play With Me

It was hurtful when no one wanted to play a quick game of hide and seek with me. "Not right now" or "Too busy," they responded. I was a young child but sitting in a recliner in front of the TV didn't look busy to me. I internalized their response to mean that I wasn't worth their time.

"Sorry kiddo, you just don't measure up."

This thought pattern and inclination to internalize what looked like unresponsiveness to my needs began way before marriage; it was born in my base nature.

In my finite knowledge, I didn't know what I didn't know about the rigors of being a homemaker to three toddlers (my brother, sister, and I). I wish I could whisper "Boo" to my mama and give her a huge repentant hug. I get it *now*. But then, as a child, after a few times of getting that response, I stopped asking because the apparent rejection and disregard for *my* needs hurt.

Much like I expected my parents to play with me whenever I requested them to, I did the same with God over the years. My expectation of God, as His child, was that He would immediately respond to my requests of Him. I was terribly disappointed with God because I felt like He was ignoring me and I did not trust Him with my heart. I stopped hoping, expecting, and asking of Him for things that I thought would nurture and bolster meaningful connection between He and I. I figured He'd get around to it when it was convenient for Him and let me know when He was ready to engage me in that way (toxic internalizing).

As I shared in the previous chapter, on many levels, what I expected from God was insulation from the troubles of this sin-stained world. Much like I would be puzzled watching my parents sit in the recliner and not play with me, I was puzzled when trouble came knocking at my door. Since God is sovereign, He clearly gave trouble my address! How could He!

I did not trust His love and care for me due to his apparent unresponsiveness to my need to meaningfully connect with Him. There was a definite external influence for my decision to run and hide from His call and it was *not* my marriage. It influenced my decision to run and hide from His call to hop on board for that piggyback ride and doubt His love. It occurred *way* before my marriage.

I was molested as a child and one of my parents walked right in on one incident and said nothing. The degree of their response did not match the degree of the event. It was all so very disorienting. I wanted to feel protected whenever the predator came around and I didn't want to be afraid so I hid from the predator as well as hid from my parents. I wasn't sure they saw me or my need. I wondered if they were powerful enough against predators in their place as my guardians. To protect and take care of myself, hiding is what I was empowered to do so, hid I did. As an adult, my hiding places became more sophisticated than under the bed, my closet or top limb of the magnolia tree but whenever I felt indefensibly vulnerable, hid I did.

I tried so hard in my young mind to solve my pain and confusion. Now, if my bed wasn't made, I didn't eat all of my veggies or ate a chocolate chip cookie ten minutes before dinner, I definitely got a swift response from my parents: the fiery fury of hades erupted on my little backside. I deduced that rule keeping, making my bed, eating all of my veggies, was far more important than my feelings of fear and being unprotected. Rule-keeping became a stronghold as I associated it with what was "right" and "trouble-free."

I applied much of the same approach with God and I believed it was the key to a "trouble-free" life. Trouble would only come as a result of my not performing according to all of the rules. I didn't want God to get mad at me and I lost any expectation that He would jump to my defense and punch my predators in the face. I hadn't earned that level of relationship yet, I thought. I just needed to remain focused on getting into less trouble and work to increase my value with Him and earn that coveted level of meaningful connection, right? Wasn't that the key?

This thinking would have been okay except the Spirit of God was alive and living in my heart, grieved by the relational distance more than I. The hurt was an indicator that God intended for our relationship to be far more than rule keeping; greater intimacy and closeness was His desire too. I needed to draw closer to Him to hear better.

I had the value and importance of rule keeping all mixed-up and backwards. To do *because* you are loved is the healthy driver for behavior, not the performance-based alternative in which you are loved *because* you do.

"We love because he first loved us" (1 John 4:19, NIV).

Responding to God's call drives us to demonstrate our trust in Him, We can do this more easily as we grow in our understanding of His love for us and incomprehensible vastness.

Trusting God and submitting our will in response to His call is what's best for us. That word submission had seriously poor associations for me but growing in my understanding of God's love helped me to know what it really means. Submission does not mean indiscriminate subjection to others. It means a demonstrated trust in a trustworthy God; you have listened and responded based on His truth and love for you. He has your best interest only at heart. He will *never* steer you the wrong way and most certainly *never* away from Himself. You only need to believe that; have faith.

As P. B. Wilson states in her book *Liberated Through Submission, The Ultimate Paradox,* "Submission without faith is slavery."

As further reflected in the verse that I shared in the introduction of this book, a proper understanding of His love is critical to seeing who God truly is and enables our ability to fully and freely relate to Him:

> There is no fear in love [dread does not exist]. But perfect (complete, full-grown) love drives out fear, because fear involves [the expectation of divine] punishment, so the one who is afraid [of God's judgment] is not perfected in love [has not grown into a sufficient understanding of God's love].
>
> 1 John 4:18 (AMPC)

Void of this progressively deepening understanding of God and His love, I was missing out on the confidence, courage, and empowerment that comes through that understanding.

It's A Family Affair

Facades or rather *masking* was another external conflict and struggle because it was like a hood that covered me, causing the restriction of my senses. It caused my blindness, deafness, muteness, and it nearly suffocated me.

As I alluded to, in the hospital event in Chapter One, I would put on a mask to deal with emotional turmoil. This ability was not something I entirely came up with by my own instinct; some of it was learned behavior from my family's way of handing emotional stuff.

I was a member of a family that suppressed any would-be displays of raw, intimate, deeply passionate emotion: "There, there now; there's no need for all that gushy stuff." We were genuine, but very proud in a way that does not express itself outwardly.

On many occasions in my life, I needed the family pride to give way to celebration, to exuberance, to some outward expression of passion. But our family pride kept it "in check." I wanted to be gushy and needed to know and feel the healthy touch of love.

We all kept an emotional lid on our feelings. It ran so deep in my veins that my prayer, praise, and worship life was parched—dry and lifeless—from its effects. I never quite seemed able to arrive at that deep place of meaningful connection. My spiritual exercises always stopped short of the intimate experience I was longing for. The torrential flow of spiritual tides that I needed to flood my soul and refresh my perspective of who I was to God always seemed to get dammed upstream, so I remained parched.

Here's an example of how this pride manifested itself after it came to light that a cousin had been molesting me. I recall a rather stately inquisition—just the facts…but no tears or hugs. So I surmised that I *should* deal with pain and frightful emotional confusion by hiding but more specifically by donning a mask.

I perceived that my own mama had done this as I recall her valiantly caring for her three children alone after my parents divorced, while trying to process her own pain, grief, and disappointment over their failed marriage. I believed she needed someone—perhaps a family member—to get down on their knees with her and help pick up the emotional pieces and get "gushy." I felt as though most (not all) around her were more concerned about keeping their own masks on. It is risky, you know, to bend down and stoop over to care enough to help another pick-up her broken pieces; your mask might fall off, too.

Maybe she cried on their shoulders behind closed doors to spare her children from seeing it. Maybe she didn't cry at all.

I didn't know about those *grown-up* things, but what I do know is that there were masks: tough exterior shells and facades.

I was often devastated from my misplaced hope that the masks would actually work—that they would insulate me from pain and emotional confusion. My strategy of wearing them to cover me was also the formula for a stress stroke; suppressing expression of my emotions and retarding their healthy development.

I didn't know how to "unplug" from seeking coverage and venture out into the open, to drop the masks and come from behind the shield and take my chances. It was a behavior pattern that ran deep. That's why I allowed so much pressure to be placed on me to keep up appearances in my very public marriage. I was practically doubled over under the weight of all those masks I was carrying! I lost nearly all ability to feel and express my feelings honestly—raw and pure. My emotional responses were aimed at convincing people I was whole rather than to mirror transparent wholeness from the abiding wisdom of God.

> "A fool gives full vent to his anger, but
> a wise man keeps himself under control"
> (Proverbs 29:11, NIV).

My misunderstanding and heretical teaching I received on this verse wreaked much havoc in my life.

Notice it says "under control" and not "silent." It is about practicing restraint not mastering the ability to live as a mute. I did not discern the difference and so my lack of understanding advanced my strategy to continue to wear masks.

My environment fostered and cultivated my ignorance. When life hurt or trouble came, I put on a mask and was certain to keep following those rules, holding out for the hope that God would eventually start insulating me after I proved myself worthy.

I had a trunk full of masks. The question for so long was not should I wear a mask but rather, which one should I wear? This behavior further deepened my sense of guilt and shame and increased the relational distance between me and God.

Helpless Defense

So, what do you do when you are faced with a condition that you are helpless to defend against it; at the mercy of it? I am sure that little Adad felt this way.

During this time of Jonah, the king of the Assyrian empire was Adad-Nirari III (811-783 BC). He had an incredible legacy to live up to seeing as his grandfather was one of the greatest Assyrian kings of all times, Shalmaneser III.

In their book titled, *Assyrian History: A Captivating Guide to the Assyrians and Their Powerful Empire in Ancient Mesopotamia*, Captivating History records the following:

> Tukulti-Ninurta II died, and he turned the kingdom—which was rapidly becoming a powerful empire—over to his son, Ashurbanipal II, who would be the 1st in a long line of Assyrian kings who are now considered to be among the most powerful and ruthless leaders in history.
>
> Ashurbanipal II, was succeeded by Shalmaneser III in 858 BCE, and his reign would be nearly entirely defined by war. In total, he found himself off campaigning and conquering for 31 of the 34 years he spent as king, a remarkable number even by Assyrian standards.
>
> In the south, though, Shalmaneser III would see far more success, as he was able to bring the city of Babylon under Assyrian control.

Little Adad had a lot riding on his young shoulders when he came into power. So young was he in fact that his mother Sammu-ramat served as regent in his stead until he became of age. I would dare say that he was defenseless against his condition; a king not old enough to wield his own vested power.

Adad's father, Shamshi-Adad V, handed down a significantly weaker Assyrian kingdom to his son, notwithstanding that he fought his brother, little Adad's uncle, for the throne. The family fight dragged on and resulted in a civil war within the empire for four years. I wonder if after Adad's father died if his uncle had any members of his lineage lying in wait for the chance at a coup d'état and assassination of little Adad. I would dare say that he was defenseless against his condition and hated for circumstances that he didn't cause.

> "…like an eagle that stirs up its nest and hovers over its young, that spreads its wings to catch them and carries them on its pinions" (Deuteronomy 32:11, NIV).

In her book *Loving and Letting Go*, Carol Kuykendall's passage on child-rearing aptly applies to how God rears us; all of His little children. She writes:

> "Letting go is a two-part process for the eagle mothers. First they 'stir up' the nest, making it less comfortable by removing layers of soft materials to reveal sharp prickly twigs that encourage the eaglet to test its wings…
>
> Then the parent eagle begins a time of training, standing by during those test

flights, fluttering over its young, spreading out its wings, catching the eaglet when it falls, patiently correcting, teaching, and encouraging it to try again. Finally, when the eaglet is capable, it flies away, strong and free and alone, ready and able to seek its potential in life because of the training it received."

Although God never *leaves* us, He allows us to hide in our comfort zone. Other times, He gently walks up behind us and whispers "Boo," revealing our finite vulnerabilities. Not that God physically plays hide and seek with us, but He does use the stuff of life including our helplessness to reveal His love and hand actively training us so that we might mature.

I can be stubborn about moving when I am comfortable, especially when nestled in the layers of my soft bedding after a warm, luxurious bubble bath. I was too *comfortable* with running and trying to stay hidden. He would eventually have to allow my aching feet and the living conditions of my hiding places to become unbearable.

God is our faithful teacher, consistently instructing us in the ways of the truth as we travel along on our journey. God is our ever-present tutor; accessible and passionately available to assist us in achieving victory for our good, the good of others, and His glory.

He lived a perfect life and endured the pain and shame of the cross just to be able to connect with us. When we respond to His call to hop on board for that piggyback ride and allow Him to escort and navigate us away from our fears, unbelief, and ish-yous, we are accepting His invitation to nurture and bolster meaningful connection with Him.

God is faithful to do His part, but we have some doing to do too: respond in faith and trust, laying our helplessness at His feet!

That is all He was asking of me and is asking of you: hop on board! He will never get weary and drop us.

But how do we let go of all of the internal and external conflicts and struggles? How do we let go of all the guilt and shame so that we can regain our senses of who our mighty and loving God is?

Let go! *Let's go!*

"*...as the Master Angler awaits our arrival on the shoreline.*

Here we go a fishin'!
The prize on the line!
Oh how exciting!
Oh how fine!"

Chapter Three

Jump Already!

> *"Nevertheless the men rowed hard to bring it to the land; but they could not: for the sea wrought, and was tempestuous against them."*
>
> Jonah 1:13 (KJV)

God loves us all so very much and He desires that we respond to His call. He wants to navigate us away from our fears, unbelief and ish-yous by directing our path. We may try to muffle His voice with our fretful striving but He continues to faithfully and patiently call to us.

The longer we delay in responding to God with a yes and hop aboard, our finite reasoning and logic tends to get the best of us and takes over the helm, directing our path. God's navigation plan for our lives is clearly taking us in the *right* direction based upon His incomprehensible wisdom, but when we turn down God's offer, we are left to strategize and rationalize our reasoning for why going the other way is a better direction than His *right* way for our life. We are also left with the consequences of journeying the lesser path.

Oh the weight and burden of directing your own life apart from God's wisdom and understanding!

> "Trust in the Lord with all thine heart; and lean not unto thine own understanding. In all thy ways acknowledge him, and he shall direct thy paths" (Proverbs 3:5-6, KJV).

I *did* want God to take away my fears, unbelief and ish-yous but I didn't want to hop aboard. Trying to figure out how to have your cake and eat it too, is a strenuous mental exercise.

So, not having a clue about what a more comfortable and familiar path looked like, I made up one as I went. First, I attempted to normalize God and bring Him down to my size, putting His ways and thoughts on the same level as mine. His Spirit living in my heart would not cooperate with my plan by keeping silent and going along with it because this strategy that I charted was not based in truth.

> For my thoughts are not your thoughts, neither are your ways my ways, saith the Lord. For as the heavens are higher than the earth, so are my ways higher than your ways, and my thoughts than your thoughts.
>
> Isaiah 55:8-9 (KJV)

> Howbeit when he, the Spirit of truth, is come, he will guide you into all truth: for he shall not speak of himself; but whatso-

> ever he shall hear, that shall he speak: and he will shew you things to come.
>
> John 16:13 (KJV)

My desire and plan was for a more comfortable and familiar path for navigating me away from my fear, unbelief, and ish-yous; I wanted the freedom and meaningful connection with God but I did not want to have to hop aboard that piggy-back ride to get it. Hoping aboard required more trust than what I was willing to give and it promised to take me out of my comfort zone.

Preoccupied Parent

Much like a child who will act out to get the desired attention of a preoccupied human parent, I reasoned that I could influence God in the same way: to let me have my way of freedom and meaningful connection without the piggy-back ride.

I began relating to God much like a baby who purposefully falls down to draw out the compassionate care of her parent. The tiny cute person is pretty skillful in working her plan because typically someone who hears the cutie go splat on the ground will drop everything for a moment and attend to the baby's needs. A child may purposefully fall down or vomit or even run straight into harm's way consciously (sometimes even at the expense of an injury) to get the parent to draw compassionately near them.

I, too, kept falling down to get an amenable response from God and His presence near me. I did feel His response to my wobbly behavior, but only one aspect of it. Seeking his attention this way was the extent of the relational capacity I opened myself up to receive from Him. I wasn't giving Him all of my heart or all of my trust; just a fragment of it and as a result, an emotional "quick fix" is all that I felt as a response from God.

God is close to the brokenhearted, noted in Psalm 34:18, and indeed I felt Him close to me in a weepy kind of way. My Heavenly Father had more than bandages for my scrapes, an ice pack for my bruises, and pity for my injuries. He wanted to teach me how to walk, run, soar, and keep from ever falling down.

How could I normalize God and make Him out to be some finite preoccupied parent? Easy, by leaning on my own understanding much like the sailors in the story of Jonah, thinking that they could row their boat to safety in a God-sized storm!

Now these hide-and-seek games that I charted to get my way was getting dangerous; it wasn't *cute* anymore. This crossed the line. God being a preoccupied parent is flatly not true.

> The LORD is my shepherd; I shall not want. He maketh me to lie down in green pastures: he leadeth me beside the still waters. He restoreth my soul: he leadeth me in the paths of righteousness for his name's sake. Yea, though I walk through the valley of the shadow of death, I will fear no evil: for thou art with me; thy rod and thy staff they comfort me. Thou preparest a table before me in the presence of mine enemies: thou anointest my head with oil; my cup runneth over. Surely goodness and mercy shall follow me all

the days of my life: and I will dwell in the house of the LORD forever.

Psalm 23:1-6 (KJV)

This finite rationale fed upon itself and grew stronger and more harmful. It was in my head and the longer I delayed in responding to God fully with all of me, the more time all of that sewage had to seep into my heart, my mind, and my ways. I was now creating an alternate reality where the truth of the character of God was concerned.

Not only had I begun to normalize the character of God but I also began to normalize His acts of grace and mercy. His acts toward us are not *normal*, they are *miraculous*. I am so grateful:

> "The LORD is gracious, and full of compassion; slow to anger, and of great mercy" (Psalm 145:8, KJV).

Try Again

As we looked at it in chapter one, Jonah hailed from the town of Gath Hepher (2 Kings 14:25) which was given as an allotment for Zebulun (Joshua 19:13) who was one of Jacob's sons; one of the twelve tribes of Israel.

Aside from God showing kindness to Leah, Zebulon's mom, and gracing her with children on account of her not being loved by her husband Jacob, an additional critical element unfolds in this family drama.

Rachel, Leah's sister was Jacob's other wife and Jacob loved Rachel though she was barren.

> "When the LORD saw that Leah was not loved, he opened her womb, but Rachel was barren" (Genesis 29:31, NIV).

In spite of the clear fact that Jacob *loved* Rachel and made even more abundantly clear that he *did not* love Leah, Leah continued to make efforts to get Jacob to love and prefer her over her sister, but to no avail! Jacob *loved* Rachel!

Rachel was barren for a good number of years and Leah surely thought that her ability to have Jacob's children would do the trick to turn his attention her direction; no such luck. Jacob *loved* Rachel.

Here is the kicker: leaning on her own understanding, Leah thought that the birth of Zebulun, their sixth son, would seal the deal to provide increased opportunity to nurture and bolster meaningful connection and ultimately relational closeness between she and Jacob. She thought he would *finally* fall for her and love her:

> Then Leah said, "God has endowed me with a good gift; now my husband will dwell with me, because I have borne him six sons." So she named him Zebulun.
> Genesis 30:20 (NASB)

The New Living Translation reads, "She named him Zebulun, for she said, 'God has given me a good reward. Now my husband will treat me with respect, for I have given him six sons.'"

I wonder if she rejected her children because they didn't provide the result she was hoping for. Were they just tools for her? Did she miss out on giving and receiving the love that relationships with children can bring? Did she take God's grace and mercy for granted? Was she even thankful to God for allowing her the awesome privilege of bearing children?

Leah had no more sons after Zebulun. Her hopes of bearing children to get her way with Jacob were dashed, much like the sailors who reasoned that throwing their cargo and livelihood overboard would provide their way to saving themselves.

Strategizing a plan apart from God's plan for me, put my spiritual disciplines on the shelf; especially my prayer life and it left me with impaired judgement; insensitive to God's guidance and voice. I grew more dense to my finite rationale which normalized my problems and consistently proved unwise and incapable of navigating me away from my ills.

The "Do-Bot" Thing!

I married at nineteen years old to the strong, silent type. I wish now that I had a man in my life who could wisely vet my fiancé and press his buttons, stir up his deep waters, and expose what lie beneath before we married.

In their book *The Two Sides of Love*, Gary Smalley and John Trent describe in great detail human temperament strengths and weaknesses by dividing them into four major categories. While mostly everyone has a mixture of the four, one is typically dominant. They write:

> (Golden Retrievers) are just like their counterparts in nature. If you could pick one word to describe them, it would be loyalty. They're so loyal, in fact, that they can absorb the most emotional pain and punishment in relationships—and still

stay committed. They're great listeners, empathizers and warm encouragers—all strong soft side skills. But they tend to be such pleasers that they can have great difficulty in adding the hard side of love when it's needed.

My dominant natural temperament is the "Golden Retriever." God gave me my temperament just as He gave you yours. The invitation that I make for God to take the helm of my life keeps my dominant bent from destroying me.

We allow God to guide us when we, by one decision at a time, do things His way, according to His Words and declared will.

Well, combine my unsubmitted dominant temperament with my uncontested dominant spouse, and voila, it turned me into a top of the line "do-bot." So what exactly is a do-bot? Well, it is similar in nature to a robot. A robot is an inanimate machine that *mimics* the behavior of a sentient, thinking being. The one who has the robot's remote control has absolute power over its operation. A "do-bot" *is* a sentient being that mimics the behavior of a robot. Those who are allowed to control it have power over its operation.

For a period in my life and marriage, that's what I became, a "do-bot." In short, anything I was asked to *do*, I 'bout did it all, without resistance. The condition of my thinking and ways worsened and grew more spiritually and emotionally dangerous; I needed help.

The sailors on board with Jonah needed help too and casting lots didn't quiet the storm though it did put them on the path for a face-to-face meeting with the creator of the storm. I was on a collision course with our compassionate God too, a face-to-face meeting of a lifetime.

> "Turn your eyes upon Jesus
> Look full at His wonderful face
> And the thing of earth, will grow strangely dim
> In the light of His glory and grace."

"Turn Your Eyes Upon Jesus" by Helen Howarth Lemmel (1922)

How unmerciful of me to subject myself to fickle, sinful people!

> "David said to Gad, 'I am in deep distress. Let me fall into the hands of the LORD, for his mercy is very great; but do not let me fall into human hands" (1 Chronicles 21:13, NIV).

Why would I do such a thing to myself? Easy, I was leaning on my own understanding, thinking that I could prove myself to God in a performance-based environment and excel in keeping all of the rules and possibly even earn some extra credit by performing acts of humility and deference in a harsh and cruel environment. Would that influence God my way?

I was so recklessly out of God's control and under the control of others I wound up doing things I did not want to do and receiving the opposite of what I wanted; I felt further devalued and lonely. I also bent myself out of shape and contorted into something other than what God made me to be.

For example, my husband would often quote that passage of scripture about "wives be submissive" and "husbands are the head." I shut my eyes, ears, and heart to the other parts of that same passage of scripture, which included so many other aspects of balance and accountability. I allowed it to be the tool to fuel my plan to influence God.

My prayerlessness and other areas lacking spiritual discipline caused my indifference toward God to grow and it plumped me up as prey for the enemy. Consequently, my "God is far too busy doing God stuff and He is not to be trifled with" ish-you went unchecked and flourished in my head and heart.

I subconsciously developed some terrible strategies of setting myself up in humiliating situations to get God's supportive attention in hopes of influencing God to accomplish what I desired. Enduring the toxicity in my marriage became a tool in my hand to prove to God how tough I was and therefore valuable and worthy of His relational closeness and embrace of me.

The Damsel In Distress—Bad Fairy Tale

Though it appeared passive, my pursuit was aggressively reckless, and I threw my white silk, lace handkerchief on the floor in an effort to get my husband to respond to me from the heart. If I could influence my husband, surely I could influence God too, right? Though as my husband, he was supposed to meet some of my needs, he was simply not designed to meet those most critical needs of my soul and spirit; only God is designed for that.

We invited a ministering couple to dine at our house. They were about forty years older than I. They graciously accepted the invitation several weeks before and were driving approximately sixty miles from a neighboring city in Massachusetts. I must admit that I felt a little pressure, given their years in the ministry, to exhibit proper etiquette and good old-fashioned manners. Being in their presence was mildly disarming. I believed that they had seen so much over their years of ministry that it created less of a need of wearing masks.

A short time before they arrived, the countertops were piled high with dishes. It looked as if we were packing up and moving out. The plan was to emerge with a clean dignified personal appearance and a tidy parsonage that we called home. Of course, ironing the table linens, setting the table, and fan-folding the napkins was a must. But attempting these simple tasks put my nerves on edge. It's not like the three children and our three dogs quietly stayed put to accommodate my efforts.

He finally arrived home less than an hour before our guests were due to arrive, freshly-shaven, cologned, and clad in new clothes. He quickly surveyed the kitchen and my personal appearance which were both in shambles and he seemed genuinely concerned.

Could it be? A glimpse of he and God being influenced my direction!

He wanted to make a good impression on our guests and getting in agreement with me was the consequence. I feasted on the crumb!

So, guess what?

He volunteered to wash the dishes to allow me to make myself presentable. He picked up my hankie off the floor! Yes!

Just as I was heading up the stairs to get ready, he asked me a question.

"What do you have planned to serve our guests?"

Being the delicate damsel I wanted to pass out. I didn't keep the main thing the main thing!

Our refrigerator was stocked with a partial stalk of semi-wilted celery, half a container of salad dressing, and some dregs of butter. The freezer had one pack of frozen chicken legs. Our shelves had one container of rice, a can of soup, and a couple of jars of seasoning, cereal, peanut butter and jelly and baby food. We also had a candy dish filled with ketchup and soy sauce packets from fast food restaurants. Bottom line, there was no food ready to prepare and all of our dishes were dirty.

I was feeling faint (at least I acted like it). I also felt my new hero-volunteer's commitment waning in the face of the myriad of tasks that needed to be completed to pull this evening off…and it was to begin in less than an hour.

Like a flash of lightning a brilliant idea popped into my light head and I peeked out from under my mask and blurted out, "Let's just take them out to eat?" He was averse to the idea, reasoning what was the use of inviting them *over* if we really weren't going to have them *over*. Our home would be the perfect setting for the deep, intimate fellowship we desired. No sooner than I agreed, another flash of lightning occurred: He blasted out the door!

"Janeen," he said, "don't stress out about cooking a large dinner. I'll just get some stuff to make a nice large salad."

His attempt at getting in agreement with me was welcomed and warmed my heart, but I had pulled out the china (of course they were the only clean dishes in the house) and set a beautiful formal dining table to invite them to drive this far for *salad*!

And guess what else the happy, eager shopper didn't do? Wash those dishes!

I could have sworn that I heard him say, "Uh-oh, sweetie, your hankie dropped" when he volunteered to wash the dishes. But he didn't pick it up off the floor! He got mud all over it when he bolted out the door.

Fifteen minutes before they arrived, I looked like the kitchen—a stressed mess! I had just lost my volunteer (knight in shining armor) and nothing was cooked. I knew our guests would be on time and that they would be walking into the midst of our crossfire.

What felt like seconds later, I heard a car crunching into our seashell-covered driveway. As folks pulled down into the driveway their headlights provided a clear view into the kitchen.

I unrealistically hoped it was him returning from the store, but deep down I knew better. In my dash to peek out the corner of the window to confirm my suspicion, I stared straight into the beam of their headlights. A blast of bright light usually triggers a migraine for me. So as I was half-blinded and stumbling about in mild pain the sound of the doorbell was like fingernails unmercifully raking across a chalkboard. Also, though I could taste some residue, I couldn't see the white toothpaste on my red lipstick because of the haloes and auras the migraine was beginning to bring on. The time I should have been spending preparing to usher them through the front door, and away from the kitchen's back door, I spent struggling to get that toothpaste glue all off.

As you might have guessed, our guests unfortunately entered through the kitchen door because I was too slow, wrestling with that toothpaste, to head them off. I was stumbling and fumbling around in such a rushed panic. As I think back on that night, I laugh myself to tears. It was like something out of a cartoon strip or episode of "I Love Lucy."

I wanted to run out of the *front* door as they entered through the *back* door. I couldn't do that, though, because I couldn't just leave them on the kitchen doorstep and pretend no one was at home after they had driven so far to visit. I also held them in high esteem.

I answered the kitchen door (in the dark) and greeted them with big hugs. I was apologetic for the kitchen while grinning like something was in my teeth.

About twenty awkward minutes later, he walked in.

What a humiliating set up!

The damsel in distress routine got me nothing! My hankie was still on the floor, and more mud was being tracked all over it.

By the way, we never saw them again.

That was a tremendous missed opportunity to grow *together* with them. They had been so helpful to us, as far as ministry was concerned. They had to be sick of us.

I was sick of my own self!

The sailors were probably sick of Jonah too because they lost so much energy being frightened and crying out to their gods and they lost so much of their resources from having thrown their cargo overboard and they certainly placed their business reputation at risk.

The sailors had no idea of just who they were dealing with. Why else would anyone lean on their own understanding? They must not know who they are dealing with; the true and living God.

As the sailors were trying to understand why the storm was happening to them and before the lot fell on Jonah, they already knew that he was running from the presence of the Lord.

> Then were the men exceedingly afraid,
> and said unto him. Why hast thou done

this? For the men knew that he fled from the presence of the LORD, because he had told them.

Jonah 1:10 (KJV)

I imagine that it was probably pretty hard to roll the dice on a ship nearly breaking from the rocking and rolling of the violent sea, but that's basically what casting lots is like. You throw the dice or object and whoever the dice or object falls nearest to is the supernatural choice, or so the sailors believed. I imagine that it was probably also hard to hear and remain settled enough to have any length of a conversation, yet in the midst of all of this, they threw the lot and it managed to clearly fall on Jonah:

> "He answered, 'I am a Hebrew and I worship the LORD, the God of heaven, who made the sea and the land'" (Jonah 1:9, NIV).

Again, using my sanctified imagination, the sailor's response in their eyes probably went something like this:

> *Uh oh! That God! The God that sent the plagues and parted the Red Sea God...the God that toppled over the walls of Jericho God...King David's God! Okay boys, we've got to get this guy back to shore! If this is what his God is doing to us by just having him onboard, imagine what will happen if we throw him overboard to a certain death. Row harder men, row harder!*

They were *still* leaning on their own understanding and risking their lives. Jonah told them to throw him overboard. He probably needed their help to make it over the side of the watery roller coaster ride.

They were now finally aware that they were witnessing a display of God's power and glory. I was on track now to do the same, but not from any out of this world display, but an equally impactful event just the same; it was through the tears of a loving and caring child.

> The LORD said, 'Go out and stand on the mountain in the presence of the LORD, for the LORD is about to pass by.' Then a great and powerful wind tore the mountains apart and shattered the rocks before the LORD, but the LORD was not in the wind. After the wind there was an earthquake, but the LORD was not in the earthquake. After the earthquake came a fire, but the LORD was not in the fire. And after the fire came a gentle whisper. When Elijah heard it, he pulled his cloak over his face and went out and stood at the mouth of the cave…
> I Kings 19:11-13 (NIV)

In the Garden

After consulting with one psychiatrist, one psychologist, and one Christian marriage and family therapist over a three-year period, we were left with the conclusion that my husband was suffering from chronic depression. Each of the professionals believed that it stemmed largely from ish-yous in his childhood that apparently began to manifest in chronic depression during the second year of our marriage and before we began having children.

In our counseling sessions, the therapists typically noted within the first half-hour that I was withstanding a considerable amount of emotional abuse. They advised me to take some measures to consider my own psychological health, to which he responded in fury. Needless to say, each of these attempts at counseling was cut short.

I had endured a lot; the verbal abuse and mind games had gotten so bad that I did things to avoid the unceasing cadence of conflict which ended up further enabling his unhealthy behavior towards me.

I made maxi-pads and diapers out of tissue and packing tape. I had panty hose with so much clear nail polish on them to stop the runs, it's a wonder the friction from even the slightest movement didn't set the church pew on fire that I sat on. My toothbrush looked like a piece of chewed sugar cane. But I accepted all of this. I endured it as a good soldier at war. At the time, the only reward I wanted was a garden. I did all the yard work anyway, so it shouldn't have been that big of a deal to get some support to make this happen.

I love the outdoors and looked forward to planting a garden with my children. My mom and grandma had gardens. I had so many good memories as I recalled and shared in my personal journaling time. I learned so many life-lessons gardening and I wanted to pass them along and share them with my children. So let the gardening begin!

It took a week to prepare the soil for our plot, and because the children had a passion to *pick* the fruit, keeping the seeds in the soil took a few extra patient but joyous days.

They were so excited, and so was I. A few weeks later, after weeding, watering, and watching, the first sprouts of our labor appeared.

Our garden eventually did so well it inspired a few ladies in the church to plant one of their own. It was bountiful and made far more than enough cherry tomatoes, cucumbers, green beans, and sunflower seeds so that we had more than enough to eat and share with others.

One evening, he assured me (as usual) that he had put our three Rottweilers away. Contrary to what he said, though, he usually left them uncaged to roam around unsupervised. I would hear them running around and climb out of bed to put them away to keep some semblance of order in the yard. On this particular night, I was too exhausted from the rigors of the day and fell asleep. To my horror, when I got up in the morning I discovered that the entire garden was dug up and scattered to bits all over the yard.

I was crushed!

It cut me deep because it felt like the little bit of family legacy I was trying to build upon and give to the next generation was cut down. That garden was going to be the springboard to begin sharing with them about their great-grandma: the traditions and love, the good stuff, and the rich memories and lessons learned under her care and tutelage. All now laying in ruin.

Quiet on the outside yet screaming on the inside, I was anguished, seething, and sorrowful. I just couldn't turn my eyes away from the destruction or mask over the deep sense of violation. I just kept mulling this over and over again in utter disbelief when suddenly my focus was snatched away by the gentle whisper of my toddler.

With tear-filled eyes she said, "Mommy, look, we can fix it," while trying to gently hold two pieces of the sunflower stems together.

> "Above all, love each other deeply, because love covers over a multitude of sins" (1 Peter 4:8, NIV).

My little child was trying to respond to *my* disappointment, with no regard for her own!

In that moment, I saw the heart of God! It broke His heart to see me hurting from my fears, unbelief, and ishyous; holding on so tightly to the very things I needed to let go of, to make room for His embrace. He yearned to navigate me away from these things as He was gently holding my brokenness. He'd done all that He could do but I needed to respond to Him! Let go! Jump aboard!

He already considered me, but I was not considering Him. He had chosen me as His very own but I needed to choose Him and His way. I definitely *never* wanted to see that look on my children's faces ever again if I had *anything* at all to do with it.

In reverential fear, I cried out to God and bowed my knee in humble submission. I cried for days. I finally came inside from the extended game of hide and seek; it had long been time to fully respond with a yes. He'd *been* calling me to come inside and enjoy the sumptuous meal He had prepared.

> "Behold, I stand at the door, and knock: if any man hear my voice, and open the door, I will come in to him, and will sup with him, and he with me" (Revelation 3:20, KJV).

Buoyant To Belly Up

  I remember going to track meets in school. My favorite event was the 440-yard dash, one circuit around the entire track. The best part was the "roll out" of the last curve! Some would finish gloriously while others would fall from glory as they "hit the wall."

  It is kind of funny to watch a track star who has "hit the wall." When the lactic acid kicks up and the oxygen gets sucked out, they slow down out of that last curve as if a bear has suddenly jumped on their back. They pump their heads and lose all form and technique, attempting to throw their bodies toward the finish line: wiggling, shaking, quaking, stumbling, just struggling along in such a graceless fashion.

  This term "hit the wall" is used to describe soldiers in training who were struggling as they neared the end of the grueling obstacle course. The last obstacle that stood between them and a short sprint to the finish line was a twelve-foot-height wall.

  The wall had a rope hanging from it that was to be used by the soldier to help them climb up and over the top of the wall. For some soldiers, the rope would cradle them as they were too exhausted to use it for anything else. For other soldiers, they missed grabbing the rope entirely because their muscles would be so fatigued that they lost control of them. Unable to slow themselves because their muscles were stuck on auto-pilot, they would run right into the wall. *Smack!* From buoyant to belly-up in the blink of an eye! It would take minutes, if not hours for their fatigued bodies to make it over that wall.

  I claimed to be a Christian yet from the many years of knowing Christ, I was not close to looking like Him. I should act like Him, think like Him, and talk like Him after all these years at least a little bit; that's the natural result of a long-term close relationship. I was nowhere near an others'-centered, servant of God with a pure, humble and loving heart.

My toddler's pure heart not only allowed me to finally see God's heartbreak for me but I could also clearly see that the root cause of my problem was *me!* I "hit the wall"! My auto-pilot behavior patterns set to cope by normalizing all that God is, along with my pain, fears, unbelief, and ish-yous, went smack!

I could now finally see that God was extending Himself to me but that I wasn't extending myself to Him. I was in turn committing this delay in responding to Him against myself. And now, I was injuring those I loved most.

Yes, it was a huge, multi-faceted mess. All of the years of toxic dumping into my head and heart and trying to pull it all apart and find an opening was like trying to find a needle in a haystack, but all I had to do was respond to His call and hop on board. Our obedient response to God places the responsibility on Him to figure out how to escort and navigate us to our destination.

I hopped aboard and it started off as a bumpy ride. I thought being meaningfully connected with Jesus would always be smooth sailing but that was not so. I really was trying my best to hold on but I didn't know what I was doing; it was all *so* new. I could see that He was holding me the entire time and I wept.

God is not going to force us to do anything though He holds everything in His hands. We must bend our knee and acknowledge Him. When we do this we align ourselves with His charted path for our life. He directs it and owns the way. He's the conductor, He is the captain, and He knows where we are going and the best way to get us to the place of safety and rest. Trust Him.

"Then call on me when you are in trouble, and I will rescue you, and you will give me glory" (Psalm 50:15, NLT).

Chapter Four

In Over My Head!

> *"So they took up Jonah, and cast him forth into the sea: and the sea ceased from her raging."*
>
> *Jonah 1:15 (KJV)*

The piggy-back ride away from my fears and unbelief started out very bumpy. He was holding me but I also needed to get used to holding on to Him too; it helped make the ride smoother.

As we began journeying together, naturally we traveled back through the pathways that landed me *at that place* of fear, unbelief and ish-yous. It was a trip down memory lane of sorts. I'd suppressed many of the details that got me here. I wasn't saying a whole lot, just taking it all in.

When God threw wind at the sea causing the fierce storm, Jonah wasn't saying a whole lot either but the sailors were making a huge fuss!

The sailors were desperate and trying their best to problem solve the life-threatening mess that they found themselves in. After the lot fell on Jonah, they knew he was running from God but they did not fully understand what that *really* meant. In effort to gain greater insight of what the root cause was, they asked five questions of the culprit Jonah.

> So they asked him, 'Tell us, who is responsible for making all this trouble for us? What kind of work do you do? Where do you come from? What is your country? From what people are you?
> Jonah 1:8 (NIV)

These five questions unearthed the answers that the sailors sought. As I mentioned, I suppressed quite a bit, but being so close to the Lord, I had new-found courage to get answers too and gain greater insight of my own. I was ready to confront all that landed me in *that place*. So, I asked myself the same five questions.

The truth of the matter soon bubbled to the surface.

For starters, my thinking was off and due to the delay in my response to God's call, some strongholds had developed. My thinking had devolved so far away from the truth of God's love for me that that was the root cause of my selective hearing and wound me up at that *place*.

In his book *Let it Go!*, Tony Evans says this:

> But the kind of bondage the Bible calls a stronghold is rooted in either our own sin, in the sin of someone else, or in the fact that we live in a sin-tainted environment. You may have been abused as a child, and as a result of the abuser's sin against you, you are in emotional bondage as an adult…

Now you may be dealing with this in sinful ways with drugs or alcohol, or by taking out your anger on someone else. But in any case, the root cause of emotional strongholds is sin—which is why any solution that doesn't address the spiritual issue is not really a solution.

First question on deck: Tell us, who is responsible for making all this trouble for us?

Like Jonah, I'd rather not say. It was evident without my words.

A Walk To Remember

It was a Sunday morning and I imagined that Dad and I would take a walk to the corner store for an ice cream cone after church.

"Mama," I said, "can you please do my hair real pretty?"

"C'mon, baby," she said. "I picked out this pretty pink bow to go in your hair that will match those pretty ruffles on your dress."

I was so excited I could hardly sit still for mama to finish gussying me up.

I was busy trying to think of what flavor ice cream to order because the corner store had so many to choose from. I was also thinking that it wasn't so much the really crunchy and sweet cones that made the trip so special. It was walking down the street, hand in hand, with my dad; just him and me.

His hands were so big and strong. He was so tall.

Sometimes as we walked, we would play a game where he would rescue me from the "evil" cracks in the sidewalk. He would swing me over the cracks in the sidewalk to safety.

Sometimes he would carry me on his shoulders part of the way. I would then pretend the ruffle on my dress was a fashionable hair wig I designed just for him.

Another special part was all the attention we got from the children in my community because most of them didn't have their dads around. A few didn't even know who their fathers were. As we strolled down the street, our neighbors and especially the bullies would know they couldn't taunt me because my daddy was with me.

I would be thinking, "Honey, just glare if you dare. I am pretty and I am with my daddy!"

I got even more excited as I thought how we would finally arrive at the counter. My daddy would say, "Baby girl, you can have whatever you want. Just pick!"

Dad would place our orders and hand over the money. The store clerk would love to see us coming because my dad always gave him a little tip for all the extra attention he gave us.

I would get three scoops, even though I knew I wouldn't be able to finish it all. I would put the leftovers in the freezer at home and eat from it through the week. It served as a gentle reminder of *my* special time, with *my* daddy.

Out the door we would stroll, hand in hand, licking our ice cream cones. I imagined dropping my ice cream when we were just a few houses away from home, and I was devastated! Not only did it get on my dress but also now I would not have my reminder snack throughout the coming week.

What would I have to remind me of our wonderful time? What would I use to mark time toward his return next week? What would I have to show off to the children in the community?

I just knew we weren't going to turn around and go back, having traveled far from the corner store. But to my surprise, my dad didn't scold me. He took his napkin and wiped the ice cream off my dress and the tears from my face and told me not to cry.

"Ah, baby girl. No problem. Are you okay? We'll just go back to the store and get another one." His kindness and patience made me feel love.

I was that daughter, or at least I wished it was so. This story tugs at my heart in a way too painful to adequately describe in writing. It unearths what I longed for from my father; meaningful connection and closeness. My supple and wanting heart that yearned for this relationship spawned diseased branches and bad fruit.

In real life, my dad left my mom, brother, sister, and me when I was a schoolgirl. My parents divorced soon after their final separation.

Every day in his absence, there were no such excursions or affectionate interludes to help shape emotional healthiness. I was left to wander alone, emotionally longing and unfulfilled.

Underdeveloped.

Deformed.

Not only was I bereft of the measure of protection and security a dad's presence provides, I did not even know how to express the immense feeling of loss. In real life, my daddy loved me but what a heartbreak and traumatic let down divorce can cause to a young child. It did for me.

How does a child explain or understand such an adult thing?

I loved my daddy *so* much!

I missed him!

And *oh my* how I needed him!

Whew! With that overwhelming flood of emotion, I took my eyes off of Jesus and washed out overboard.

As I struggled in the crashing waves, slapping at the water, gasping desperately for air, I ingested a lot of sea. The salty water made me sick and a little delirious. It was beautiful, crystal clear water but not suitable for me to drink. Everything that looks good for you is not always actually good for you. My will was certainly engaged to finish this trip, but that alone was not enough; I needed to reorient myself to total dependence on God and not myself. I was in critical condition and in need of His healing in so many areas and it provoked an unfiltered, knee-jerk response from me: "Jesus!"

He responded immediately; well, actually, He was responding the whole time but I didn't realize from the behavior patterns that I'd formed that I was not only frantically swatting at the waves, but I was swinging at Him as He tried to extend His hands to continue escorting and navigating me away from *that place*. He knew everything about me and patiently helped me back on board. I was so sorry for swinging at Him.

God loved me and cared about every single detail of my life. He demonstrated it in these moments. On we continued as He carried me further away to the place of safety and rest.

I am so grateful that He is ever with me, loving me through it all.

"What kind of work do you do?" was the second question the sailors asked Jonah, to unearth the reason for the life-threatening mess they found themselves in. As a child of God, our answer to this question is pretty clear:

> "Jesus answered and said unto them, This is the work of God, that ye believe on him whom he hath sent" (John 6:29, KJV).

Not believing was another facet of my devolved thinking and reason for why I wound up in *that place*.

A Walk In My Shoes

I was so young during my first marriage, and we were both trying to figure this whole marriage thing out and define which roles and responsibilities were whose.

I placed my husband on the throne of my life with a crown and a scepter. The outfit looked good on him during the "honeymoon" period, but it faded quickly and lost its luster as the wedding officially ended and the marriage began—which came during the first few weeks of our third anniversary. Something about having a *daddy lord* over me made me feel safe and secure.

He enjoyed it. He was the king and getting the hang of wielding his scepter. As the queen, I was still adjusting my tiara. We both thought that was how things were "supposed to be." It was cute, I thought.

"Janeen, honey, get off the phone. Let's go here or there or let's participate or not," he would command. He totally dominated and I thought it was wonderfully wild.

I remember vividly the day I offered *him* the throne to my life.

He was in the US Navy and he came home one day from the ship he was serving on and told me that we were going, *right now*, to buy me a pair of shoes. My shoes had a hole in the bottom.

I felt ashamed really at my need and tried to convince him that I would be all right and that we should just save the money instead of spend it on "little old me." He was confused at my response to his command because this image of a soft, indecisive, and extremely passive Janeen is not what he knew me to be.

Nonetheless, at that moment, strong, independent, and progressive adjectives previously tied to my reputation, immediately became who *I was*.

I reasoned that we shouldn't go but he wouldn't take no for an answer and further told me to get ready because we were going to the shoe store *now*.

I remember being disagreeable with him in the store and trying to put on airs as if there was nothing in the store that would suit my taste or style. The truth was that I hadn't been in a shoe store that sold "good" shoes in so long that it was just an emotionally weird feeling. I had worked in clothing stores in high school and college and had not been in the position of having to depend on someone to completely meet my physical needs in a few years.

I was also accustomed to the southern California wardrobe—living year-round in cheap sandals and shorts. But all of that was in my past now. Winter was looming in my new New England home and I had to adapt immediately. My need for shoes had to be addressed!

I was so confused about what I was feeling as I stood in that shoe store. I was angry, ashamed, and in denial that I was shaking in my boots at my new position of dependence on *him*. I had looked for work, to no avail, which left me feeling and believing that I was useless and helpless. We didn't have a car, and their public transportation didn't compare to what I was used to in southern California (if it could be compared at all).

I was not equipped nor prepared to dig deep enough to analyze all this emotion gushing out of me in the shoe store.

I accepted the shoes and he paid for them at the register. I hastily reached out for the bag. He took it from me and told me to throw the shoes I had on away, and from the look on the face of the cashier, I knew I should have.

In attempt to salvage control of my physical needs, I told him that it would be good just to keep the old shoes so as not to wear out the new ones. He was reluctant, but he accepted that and insisted that while we were out in public, I should not wear those holey shoes.

"Janeen, put those old shoes in the bag and put on the new ones *now*, please!"

So instead of handing them over to the cashier, I put those old shoes in the box and carried them out of the store in the bag.

I felt so ashamed on the way back home. Why? My devolved thinking lost sight of the reality that God is absolutely my provider. My husband spied my vulnerability as an opportunity to lord over me. He tested his authority by making me often jump over hurdles when I needed something from the store.

In truth, I nearly demanded the hurdles because they made me feel like I earned it and was worthy of the physical provision I credited him with providing for me. These hurdles were simple at first. He wouldn't pick up his clothes off the bedroom floor after changing or in the bathroom after a shower and I would do it. Then he would no longer scrape his plate let alone take it in to the kitchen nor offer to help with the dishes at all.

I took care of things and picked up the slack with no questions asked. No moan, no groan, no gripe. I would raise no objection nor challenge him at all! Neither did the inconvenience it sometimes caused me matter at all. It did not even warrant consideration; instead of feeling deserving or worthy, I continued to feel rejected and abandoned.

I jumped over each hurdle that came up, no matter how much strain it caused me, but the prize of meaningful connection was always just out of reach. I kept running and jumping for him, but with each step I abdicated the rights to my own life

Somewhere, I stopped believing that God was my provider. Was it when my uncle brought us food boxes from his church's pantry when I was in fifth grade, because we had nothing to eat? Was it competing and winning a spot on the cheer squad but sitting on the sidelines all season watching each formation one gal short because I couldn't afford the uniforms or training camp? Was it missing out on a few school field trips or my best friend's pizza party because I didn't have the money? Not sure where exactly but somewhere it was lost and I stopped believing that God was my provider. He must have been too busy with more important things.

"*Where do you come from?*" was the third question the sailors asked Jonah. I forgot that I came from the cool kids' club because I dropped my membership card along the way to *that place* and lost it.

Cool Kids Club

Ratsah is a Hebrew word used about fifty-four times in the Old Testament. It means "to be pleased with" and is often translated as "accepted," "delighted in," and "pleasure."

Ratsah was used as God regarded something positively:

> "And he shall put his hand upon the head of the burnt offering; and it shall be

accepted for him to make atonement for him" (Leviticus 1:4, KJV).

"The Lord taketh **pleasure** in them that fear him, in those that hope in his mercy" (Psalm 147:11 KJV).

Ratsah was also used as God regarded something negatively:

> Ye said also, Behold, what a weariness is it! and ye have snuffed at it, saith the Lord of hosts; and ye brought that which was torn, and the lame, and the sick; thus ye brought and offering: should I **accept** this of your hand? Saith the LORD.
> Malachi 1:13 (KJV)

"He **delighteth** not in the strength of the horse: he taketh not **pleasure** in the legs of a man" (Psalm 147:10, KJV).

It is my strong belief that all of humanity has a longing to feel the acceptance and approval of God. Seeing as He has written His name on our hearts, we innately desire meaningful connection with Him (Genesis 2:7). His affirmation connects our spiritual reality to our earthly experience. It keeps us from feeling rejected and abandoned; it makes us feel whole.

> My son, despise not the chastening of the LORD; neither be weary of his correction: For whom the LORD loveth he cor-

recteth; even as a father the son in whom he delighteth.

Proverbs 3:11-12 (KJV)

What made me acceptable and pleasing to God was not my being perfect, but my being *willing*—willing to bring my being under the subjection of God's rule with each personal decision that I made.

"Jesus answered and said unto him, If a man love me, he will keep my words: and my Father will love him, and we will come unto him, and make our abode with him" (John 14:23, KJV).

To be found acceptable and pleasurable to God truly is a miracle of God's grace!

Ratsah is extreme. Our need to get it from God is extreme, and the cost God paid to make it available to us is extreme; for it is only by the grace of God through the sacrifice of His Son on the cross and accepting His gift of His righteousness bestowed upon us, that we are *ratsah* to God!

I believe that all human beings seek *ratsah* from God, whether their pursuit is conscious or subconscious. I see it as the "it" that people spend themselves to find. They go to bars and nightclubs, risk lying, cheating, and stealing in their own efforts to attempt to get their need for *ratsah*, satisfied through the affirmation of people or even through their own self proclamation. They sacrifice themselves to almost any object in hopes of laying hold of "it."

Weekend after weekend, day after day, they fail. All of their efforts ultimately fall short. To be found pleasurable by anything other than God does not provide the same depth of satisfaction as *ratsah* from God Himself.

I am accepted by God! He accepts all of His children!

"W*hat is your country?*" was the sailor's fourth question to Jonah.

For me, that means back to revisit Loner-Ville again.

A Walk In The Park

"Let's do lunch," was the cavalier remark made by a friend that I hadn't seen since high school. I went to visit my mama at her home in southern California—alone—for a long overdue visit and vacation. I had actually gone to recuperate because I was mildly injured in a car accident in New England.

The first couple of days, I slept.

It was wonderful and strange. The days and nights just kind of ran together. And it took me forty-eight hours just to adjust. It was hard to believe there was no one around trying to breach the quarters of my personal space.

When I finally emerged rested, my mom suggested that I get in touch with some of my old friends. So I caught up with a few of them and some girls and I went out to dinner.

What should have been an evening full of giggles, grins, and photo-ops turned out to be traumatic. I had been too isolated for too long in my little New England hometown. I was sorely unprepared for interacting with "young progressing adults" in the big, urban city.

For starters, I remember when my gal pal came to pick me up, I did not even know what kind of car she was driving. At my question of the make and model of her car, she thought I was just being "crazy old Janeen" from *back in the day*. But I really didn't know.

How did I get here? Had I been in a coma?

To see the girls again and hear their stories of life after being married with children or even the stories of those who chose the single life in corporate America, unsettled me. Although I had maintained the same dress size I wore in high school and many of them had not, they all appeared far better on the inside to me; connected and centered.

Then the moment I had dreaded shot me right between the eyes. I wanted to run away and duck down and hide when they asked me what my life was like and if I was happy. My response? I burst out into hysterical laughter near the point of tears. They then chimed in with laughter and joking. One said, "I thought when I was going to see you tonight, girl, you were gonna be wearing a habit." Oh, the depth of the unintended pun.

They thought my laughter was borne of strength. They assumed the reason I still had my high school figure was that I had made a personal commitment to myself. They thought my non-responsiveness was a gentle teasing at them.

I hit the "dress size" mark! So on the outside, it looked as though I was strong because that was *all* they could see. Unfortunately, as they continued trying to fill in the blanks, I realized that the *outside* was all they ever truly saw. My preteen and teen habits of masking kept them from seeing me and disabled them from discerning my need now. It wasn't their fault that they did not know.

Unfortunately, they assumed that their question needed no verbal answer. So they did not press for one. My physical appearance was a sufficient response to their query—so they thought. But, oh, I really felt a need to share my life experiences with "the girls." I wanted to fume, cry, and scream! I wanted to "let it out"! I wanted to purge myself of the truth about how low my self-worth and esteem had plunged. I wanted to release it.

I wanted them to help me dig out of the emotional hole I had burrowed into. I wanted them to pray for me and surround me with love to help me acquire the courage to choose faith and trust and stop choosing fear. I wanted them to accept me where I was. But I refrained. I donned the stately mask that I knew they would like and had known me for. That was sadly and painfully the only "Janeen" they had ever really known.

But I know that my laughter-to-tears was a result of their question's undoing me. I was weak. I was broken. They thought my figure was the gauge of my strength when it was really an indicator of my level of devolved thinking.

I had maintained the same dress size in part because I had "controlled" my eating. I was so afraid of being found in need of an entire wardrobe let alone shoes and I wanted to avoid vulnerability to manipulation in this area. I was growing tired of the hurdles and wanted to avoid them, so I maintained control of my size at an almost reckless pursuit by "conditioning" myself.

I remember learning about "conditioning" in a psychology class. Consistent, sustained conditions can create behavior that is predictable, automatic, performed without thought: "auto pilot." Engaged thinking and processing does not occur until the conditions are changed.

For example, if a stray kitten found a bowl of milk at 5:00 p.m. every day at my back door, come rain or shine that kitten would be found there at my back door purring for milk at 5:00 p.m. The kitten may even starve to death if after days I did not set the milk out for it. Hopefully, this change of events of not putting milk out at 5:00 p.m. would cause the kitten to get out of the "auto pilot" mode and hunt.

Anyway, I began to apply this "conditioning" to myself to control my size. When I would get hungry and was feeling that my clothes were a little too snug, I would eat ice. The process of placing the ice in my mouth and biting, chewing, and swallowing caused my brain to communicate to the rest of my body that I had just ingested food.

For about twenty to thirty minutes, my stomach wouldn't growl, and after that time expired I was always preoccupied with tending to the children, feeding, or cleaning, that when my glucose level demanded "real" attention, I was busy enough to suppress my dietary needs.

As with many women, I had low iron and I craved ice because of it. I was so miserable I would go through a ten-pound bag of ice every four days. When there was no bag of cubed ice in the house, I would take a hammer and crush the ice I'd made by filling water into a plastic sandwich bags. I knew I had a problem. My dentist told me that my teeth, albeit straight and white, had been eroded to the size of someone nearly triple my age. I cannot even begin to tell you of all the headaches and migraines I triggered due to the extreme chomping.

Pica is the name of this condition. It is defined as the compulsion to swallow non-food items. It is derived from the Latin word for the magpie bird which is known for eating indiscriminately. *Pagophagia* is the type of pica I had. Some doctors say it is the result not the cause of iron deficiency while others say it is the cause. While the earlier form of my condition was directly related to an iron deficiency, it became a psychological condition. I needed help and healing.

The final and fifth question they asked Jonah was, *"From what people are you?"* For me, that would be the group of masked people that live far and wide, from every walk of life, on the face of the earth, not just the group that birthed me.

In my devolved thinking, I began to look through the eyes of my husband, "the girls", my family, parishioners and others which in and of itself is not entirely unhealthy, it's just that their view is imperfect and incomplete. I wound up losing sight of myself as being complete and whole in Christ. I allowed their perspective to skew my judgement and box in my perspective, subsequently imprisoning my behavior.

Lady Grace

As the "pastor's wife," for years I sat alone near or on the front pew in the sanctuary. As attendees filed out of the church at the close of the service, I would often stand by his side at the back door and see them out—smiling, hugging, encouraging, and laughing all the while...*alone*. Most of my attempts to have a personal relationship with "the girls" in the congregation were foiled by their inability to see me separate from the Pastor.

One lady in the church told me, "If I went with you to the mall I would feel like I was shopping for lingerie with "the Pastor." Initially I was hurt by this distinction of separation but over time it turned to bitterness. It took time to resolve that bitterness, too.

I accepted "their way" of relating to me and enabled their thinking by putting on my "Lady Grace" preacher's wife mask.

My upbringing fostered the idea of church members being an extended family. This was absolutely *not* the perspective of the parishioners in my new hometown. We were in a New England state with a large Roman Catholic presence; fewer than two in one hundred were "evangelical

Christians". The traditions some held onto made for a tough social transition when they joined our non-denominational, Baptist-affiliated church.

At times I would see them struggling between "father" and "pastor" when they were addressing him. So, as you might imagine, those members definitely could not bring themselves to see me as "one of the girls." They were too busy processing and coming to terms with their feelings of illegitimacy regarding "their pastor" being married.

Then there were the members who were new to church life altogether. At times all the "professional" churchgoers made them so uncomfortable that they didn't know whether to bow, bend, or make direct eye contact as they addressed me. They were far too careful trying to determine an "acceptable" manner.

As they saw me providing administrative support and teaching in the women's, children's, and music ministry they concluded that I was a "helpmate suitable" but still couldn't seem to loosen up enough, to see me as one of "the girls."

I should not have allowed their response to keep me in that glass house. I was craving companionship and I got careless with handling my need.

Dr. Charles Stanley has a fantastic acrostic to help assess your condition. Regardless of what people you are around, you should always be self-aware, at all times.

Silence all of the turmoil and H.A.L.T.: never get too hungry, never get too angry, never get too lonely and never get too tired. I had a check in every box and was on track to make some very poor, costly decisions.

In his book *Getting Closer to God*, Erwin Lutzer says this:

> Where we turn when we are desperate speaks volumes about where we are in our

walk with God. Whether we draw closer to God or turn away from Him depends on how well we know Him. When we feel that God has failed, an idol stands ready to deliver us. The closer we are to God the closer we want to get; the farther we are from Him the more attractive idols become.

Walking The Plank

During that visit to my mama's house, I also got a chance to see a few of my sister's friends—the "big kid's friends." They came to visit me at my mama's house. It had been several years since I'd seen them and it was refreshing.

My grandmother's house was the "hang out" house and it's where we lived during my pre-teen and teenage years. My mama was always so welcoming to our friends and kids from our neighborhood so the house was always teeming with kids!

One neighbor in particular kept in touch with my mama and got in touch with me at her house. He wanted to see me.

The phone rang and my heart raced when I saw his name flash in the caller identification screen. I was so excited to hear from my old neighbor. The sound of his voice was like a time machine that flung me back to that skinny cheerleader I used to be in high school.

I had forgotten all about her and wasn't sure that I wanted to remember who she was. When I said "I do" in marriage I buried her, or so I tried to. I thought that that was necessary for being a good Christian wife.

At any rate, this entire vacation so far was just what the doctor ordered. When he invited me to have dinner, I admit I was looking forward to traveling down more of those familiar memory lanes.

Nostalgia, as I shall refer to him, married about two years before I did. I was confident that the time we would spend together would be relaxing and "safe." Oh, the stories and events he witnessed as *our* neighbor which made for a lot to reminisce about.

Well, there we were dining on some great authentic Mexican food (which I had been craving, since I moved away from Southern California) and having a great time recalling the "good ole' days." You see the power of this friendship was just that—we were just friends. Never an intimate hug or kiss between us.

He and I spent time together largely because we were neighbors. He lived down the street. He was within a year or so of my older sister's age and we all went to the same high school; he was like a big brother to me.

He could come over while I would have a male visitor over and his presence caused no friction at all because everyone knew the nature of our friendship. He did not have to be invited over, as legitimate suitors did (*that was a must!*).

When I didn't have an escort to a party or was just plain bored, we'd go out. We both enjoyed dancing. And dance we did 'til the curls were sweat out of my hair. Broken down cars or motorcycles were against my self-imposed social protocol, but his were so much fun to ride and push. Well dinner was nearly over when like a lightning flash came the question that I had tried to dodge from "the girls" the night before.

"So, Janeen, tell me...are you happy?"

I couldn't compose my stammering tongue. So I just cooled down and kept my composure, smiled, donned my mask, and sat there as he offered his speculation.

As he began to measure how he thought my husband *should* be treating me against the standard I required of all my teen suitors those years ago, I tasted something weird in my mouth.

Blood.

I was nibbling on the inside of my jaw so hard I was bleeding. So I readjusted my slipping mask, sipped my cola, and kept my cool. I affixed the mask tighter, just as I did every time I was confronted with potential emotional turmoil and confusion.

I finally mustered the courage to look up from my soda glass, now dry of every trace of condensation, as his "investigative reporter" style questioning ended. It was quiet for a moment or two, and I had committed to look up, on the count of three, unmoved and confident.

When I did, I found him staring at me.

Warnings flashed again!

His gaze was different; he knew it and I did, too.

Was it the blinding glare of the lights reflecting off the water drops I had been concentrating on clearing from the outside of my glass that fuzzed my vision? Was the image of the little girl left longing in my childhood there in those droplets, or did I see her needs being met in the reflection of his eyes? Could he wipe the tears away and redeem the time I had spent paying the price that my search for affirmation and meaningful connection had cost me?

We immediately called it a night and parted company. We didn't see each other again for a couple of years after that date—a reunion that would prove bittersweet.

Jonah responded to the five questions that the sailors asked of him, with one summary statement: "He answered, "I am a Hebrew and I worship the LORD, the God of heaven, who made the sea and the land" (Jonah 1:9, NIV).

In essence, in the midst of this cataclysmic storm raging in his life and now also in the lives of those in closest proximity to him, he was saying "I'm a child of the true God."

No matter where you've run and hidden or how far you think you may have run from God's call, He is still faithfully and patiently calling you. No matter how far devolved your thinking may be or how you wound up at *that place* you found yourself in, you are His accepted, beloved child and He is holding you in the palm of His hand.

Won't you hop aboard? He's pleading. He's waiting. He loves you. He wants to help you and heal you. He wants to escort you to a place of safety and rest.

> "Softly and tenderly Jesus is calling
> Calling for you and for me;
> See, on the portals He's waiting and watching,
> Watching for you and for me
>
> Come home, come home
> Ye who are weary come home
> Earnestly tenderly Jesus is calling
> Calling, O sinner, come home!"
> "Softly and Tenderly" by William Lamartine Thompson (1880)

Chapter Five

Let Me Help You!

> *"And said, I cried by reason of mine affliction unto the* LORD, *and he heard me; out of the belly of hell cried I, and thou heardest my voice."*
>
> Jonah 2:2 (KJV)

Tough Nut To Crack

Christmas time is the most wonderful time of the year, for me and many others. It is when we take the time to acknowledge the birth of our Savior and enjoy fellowship with friends and family from near and far.

As a little girl, one holiday thrill was being able to use a shiny utensil, the nutcracker. I felt like such a *big girl!* It was the coolest thing to watch the process of cracking a nut open. It was especially exciting because they were going to be used to make our holiday version of chocolate chip cookies with fresh walnuts; yes, bring on the nutcracker!

Sometimes I needed a little help with the utensil. I was too weak to apply the pressure needed to crack the walnut open and reveal what was most useful on the other side of the hard shell. At other times and to my surprise, the little pressure that I could muster would crack and crumble the entire walnut and shell to bits because it was too brittle. Its brittleness was only revealed after the pressure was applied. Then, at other times, after exerting great effort, my exhilaration quickly turned to a letdown when after the shell finally cracked open, a rotten walnut was revealed. Its rottenness was only revealed after the pressure was applied.

In the previous chapter four, I shared the major external influences that landed me at that place of fear and unbelief. These influences were only able to last for all of those years in my life because they were attached to something anchored deep on the inside of me. As I briefly discussed in chapter one, there is *something* in us that is enticed by wandering the lesser, godless path.

> When tempted, no one should say, 'God is tempting me.' For God cannot be tempted by evil, nor does he tempt anyone; but each person is tempted when they are dragged away by their own evil desire and enticed.
> James 1:13-14 (NIV)

My marital turmoil, though theatrical in scale at times, was just the shiny utensil that God used to apply the right amount of pressure and reveal not only the vulnerable, injured, and useful parts of me but also the rotten, hardened, and brittle. It revealed not only my devolved thinking but also the work that I could do to close the distance in my relationship with God.

Though it is tempting to make assumptions and draw conclusions about what Jonah was thinking when he appeared to be sullen and silent, one thing is certain; he did finally crack under the pressure of affliction that he was experiencing and responded in obedience to the Lord's call.

> "It was good for me to be afflicted so that I might learn your decrees" (Psalm 119:71, NIV).

Yes, affliction is like a nutcracker; it applies pressure in our lives to reveal what's on the inside of us. You can't ignore affliction when it comes calling, no more than when the wind blows your hair wildly out of place; it forces you to take notice. Affliction can amplify the work that we can and need to do, to close the relational distance between us and God. More importantly, affliction provides a personal, experiential lesson about who God is; His holiness and His love.

Affliction does God's bidding as it exposes our vulnerability and finite nature. It uncovers our need for dependence on God to sustain our life.

> "Man that is born of a woman is of few days and full of trouble" (Job 14:1, NIV).

> "I have told you these things, so that in me you may have peace. In this world you will have trouble. But take heart! I have overcome the world" (John 16:33, NIV).

This world is fallen, it is not paradise. Trouble will come. God knows, sees and understands it all and does not want us to go it alone; without Him. He wants to be our strong confidant and provide His divine guidance and to help us through it.

> "Many are the afflictions of the righteous: but the LORD delivereth him out of them all" (Psalm 34:19, KJV).

Victim Sketch

Jonah was a victim of sorts; he was thrown into a sea which was raging so fiercely, that well-trained, professional sailors were in fear for their life. We know the story so it can be hard to feel sorry for Jonah because we can see that he brought this situation upon himself.

Often when thinking of a victim, we are sympathetic and do feel sorry for them and justifiably so, but victims are sinners, too. Not that they are culpable, responsible, or even deserving of the actions that others have assaulted them with, but they are sinners in a way that is separate from that context of the assault and harm that they experienced.

> "…for all have sinned and fall short of the glory of God…" (Romans 3:23, NIV).

Without a doubt, I was a victim in my marriage but I was a sinner too. In God's incredible mercy, He allowed my healing to progress in such a way that I was able now to see and handle the conviction of my own sin. My sin had to be addressed because it was the something that the external factors and struggles were able to anchor to and take me for a ride to *that place*

Let's fast forward to the last chapter in the story of Jonah, to help us see how God uses affliction to help us learn our place in this world and our place in His heart.

In chapter four of his Bible story, we find Jonah delivered from the belly of the big fish. He has completed the task of carrying out God's request of him to preach to the Ninevites and he is now sitting back, watching for what he hopes will be God's wrath fall upon the Ninevites.

As Jonah was waiting to see what would become of the Ninevites, God caused the following situations to afflict Jonah. Why? To reveal the hardness in Jonah's heart that could be fixed by him repenting of it. This act of repentance would also close the distance in his relationship with God. We can't reach our full potential and be our best without God. It is our sin that hampers this.

> "I am the vine; you are the branches. If a man remains in me and I in him, he will bear much fruit; apart from me you can do nothing" (John 15:5, NIV).

God was definitely trying to get Jonah's attention and provoke him to address the stuff that was in their way relationally.

The Interlinear Bible says that God *appointed* a plant to shade Jonah and deliver him from his misery (Jonah rejoiced over that), but then God *appointed* a female scarlet worm to strike the plant and it dried up (Jonah said nothing to that). Then after the sun came up that God *appointed*, God *appointed* a scorching wind and struck the sun on Jonah's head (Jonah fainted and asked God to take his life).

You can only know what's in a tube of toothpaste after you squeeze it and God was using affliction to put the squeeze on Jonah.

When affliction comes, trust God! Admitting the hardness of your heart and obediently responding to His call will benefit you every time.

As affliction captivates our attention, affliction provokes an immediate, unfiltered, unmasked response. It exposes our private thought life which is immediately revealed in the choices that we make in those first moments that affliction strikes.

Throwing My Weight Around

I wonder what God thinks when we attempt to exert our will against His. I remember as a kindergartener catching a butterfly and putting it in an old glass jar but then letting it go within a short time because it wouldn't settle into its new home.

That butterfly was beautiful but didn't seem too smart because it kept wildly flapping and bumping into the glass as it was trying to force its way to freedom. I could empathize with the butterfly because I knew what it was like to experience pain and frustration as a result of trying to muscle into getting your own way.

Yes, kindergarten was a time of new experiences and life lessons. What I enjoyed most was the increased independence, especially riding the bus with the *big kids* to school, carrying my very own aluminum lunch pail, and having an older sister with me. This is one my earliest discoveries of the hardness that lurked in my heart.

I was on the morning half-day schedule and my sister, who was a fiery second grader, attended school all day. By the time I was waking up from my afternoon nap, she would be returning home from school.

I so looked forward to her homecoming because I wanted to hang around her and the other *big kids* on our block. I thought that was living life to the fullest!

The problem would arise for me when playtime was over. It would be time to return home but I wasn't finished playing yet! On more than one occasion, she would have to deal with the more tangible expression of my hard heart, which boldly manifested itself as a strong will. With a few missing teeth she would call out very loudly her spirited description of my stubborn display, "Janeen, you are so hardheaded!"

"Janeen, it is time to go home and eat dinner," she would demand authoritatively. The right to make authoritative demands of me was bestowed upon her at my birth. (Hey, there are just certain rights that come with being the oldest.)

"No, I'm still playing!" I would respond sharply. "I don't want to come home with you right now!"

This reply always gave me an audience of "oooohs" from the *big kids*.

They were *not* "oooohing" because I was a *big kid* too who could boss others around, order my own world, and command the attention of my peers. They were oooohing because they knew my mama! My mama "didn't play that" childish back talk display thing.

"Okay Janeen." She would snap back at me, "But you're gonna be in big trouble."

My fair-weather peer group would "ooooh" very dramatically once again, mocking my display of power and independence.

She would leave very frustrated only to return in fewer than five minutes with these fateful words: "Mama said you better come home with me or she's coming over here to get you herself!" In other words, what my sister was saying was, "Mama is going to afflict you to reveal your hard heart. What are you thinking, Janeen?"

Hmm, okay, let me think about this for a moment.

I would be so angry—not at her who was only trying to intimidate me to good works by her firm demand; she was just the messenger. What I was really mad at was my resentment at being given a choice that was really no choice at all. I wanted the best deal out of this situation. I wanted to come home when I was good and ready and I wanted my mama to lovingly accept this arrangement.

Besides, I wasn't hungry anyway.

The harder she pleaded and tugged on me to come home with her, the more I pleaded and tugged in the opposite direction. The struggle typically ended with me sitting down on the ground.

That's right, I would simply park my bottom on the ground.

My oldest sister was a cute little girl with a featherweight body frame. I was rather chunky and cute, with a brick-solid frame. Once I sat down, she could in no way move me.

She loved me and she would cry when I refused to come with her. I wanted to think that she was upset because my little fanny would pay a dear price for my folly, but on the contrary. You see, along with my mama's edict for me to come home was the promise that my sister would be in trouble if she returned home without me!

Well, the ending of this duel was not a scene of the warm and fuzzies. In brief, my mama came to get me and applied the board of education to my seat of knowledge.

Why didn't I defer to my sister's plea? What could have *possibly* gotten in the way of my ability to make a better decision? It's not like I doubted there would be consequences.

> "Foolishness is bound in the heart of a child; but the rod of correction shall drive it far from him" (Proverbs 22:15, KJV).

Whatever choice is presenting itself as a better choice than God's way is vain and really a "pseudo-choice." My mama had every right to demand my presence at the dinner table. She knew I needed to eat and all the other champions of positive growth associated with her request. Why was I so willing to self-destruct just to feel sovereign over my choices? My ego felt pretty good but my rump didn't fare so well.

I knew better! My mama had proven that she would appoint the rod to afflict me on my backside to force me to take notice. A disobedient child is a danger to themselves. Stubborn sin is in our nature and affliction is beyond our control. The longer we leave our sin unresolved, the harder our hearts can grow, requiring greater pressure to force us to take notice.

Meek Bubbles

When I was a little girl growing up in sunny southern California, I learned a song during Christmastime. Although it was great entertainment for me, it utterly disgusted my mama. The song started with: "Jingle Bells, Batman smells, Robin laid an egg." Do you remember that desecrated version of an otherwise joyous Christmas jingle?

Anyway, my mama told me not to sing that "filthy" song anymore. Much as I tried not to sing it, I continued. It was no mystery why I continued to sing it. I simply didn't want to submit my strong-will under her control.

My mom promised me that if I sang that song again, she would wash my mouth out with soap. Well, even though I believed her, I sang it again. In her shock at my obstinate belting of this tune again, she looked at my dad in utter amazement. She asked me why I would sing that song again knowing what my disobedience would bring. I told her, "I don't know."

Perhaps suspecting that I was suffering a bout of temporary insanity, she let me *slide*. She restated her promise to me, but again I had the strong-will gumption to sing *that* song!

I tried to place my hand over my mouth and stop the sound melodiously flowing out of my face, but it didn't work. She looked at my dad in amazement again! She promised and pleaded that her patience would only allow for this last *accident*, but that was it! If I dared sing it again, she would not only wash my mouth out with soap but spank my little bottom.

My younger brother made a side-eye at me, not particularly pleading with me not to do it but saying loud and clear with his non-verbal, "Good grief, Janeen is getting ready to do it again and for the life of me, I can't figure out why."

Yes, affliction was certain if I did it again, but would I? *Okay, let me think about this for a moment...*

Well, it was quiet for a few tense moments and then, all of a sudden, to everyone's surprise, out came "Jingle Smells" again. I made a dashing attempt to cover my mouth, but it came little too late. As promised, I was escorted to the restroom and received the promised mouth full of soap and the spanking. I must say that once again, she appropriately applied the board of education to my seat of knowledge.

Why would I do it knowing full well what was coming my way? I have a little sin problem as all of us do and it was revealed.

> "For the good that I would I do not: but the evil which I would not, that I do. Now if I do that I would not, it is no more I that do it, but sin that dwelleth in me" (Romans 7:19-20, KJV).

We are afflicted by our own sin. Isn't that a helpless feeling; being out of control? There are times when we surprise even ourselves with our own sinful foolishness.

We are in control of our decision making and when affliction strikes, it reveals *what we value*.

Miss Entrepreneur

Growing up in a Los Angeles County suburb afforded me quite an experience and exposure to many ethnic and socioeconomic groups. The lower-to-middle class elementary school that I attended was predominantly African-American but had a noteworthy Hispanic, Asian, and Caucasian presence.

As a sixth grader I, like most of my classmates, gravitated toward the fads of the day. During that time a particular name-brand school supplies and stationery was all the rage. They had branded pens, pencils, paper, backpacks, and the typical accompanying novelties geared toward children—

all at a steep price for parents! Their *hot* item was the scented pencils and erasers.

The only place around that sold these goods was a shopping mall several miles away. Most of my classmates' parents had not the time, means, or desire to travel such a distance to purchase these novelty items; and they comparison-shopped the competition for a better deal. It made better sense to purchase the less expensive competition sold locally. Nonetheless, the *name brand* product was coveted in my elementary school.

I remember going to this particular mall on the weekend with my allowance money of $5.00 and purchasing a few grape-, cherry-, and sour apple-scented pencils and erasers. I couldn't wait to get to school on Monday. Minutes if not seconds after pulling them out of my back pack and placing them on my desk, I was the center of attention and all but six children in the class ran over to ask me if they could use one of my pencils or erasers.

I enjoyed all of the attention and lent out one or two. By the end of the day, I had a waiting list of potential users for the next day. I did the only thing I could think to do: I ran home and waited for Mom to get home so I could ask her to advance me my allowance. *Cha-ching!* I had to get to that mall quick to increase my inventory and social standing.

I had a heart, so I let one underprivileged and socially alienated girl take a pencil home, to help her elevate her social status with the promise to return it the next day. And wouldn't you know what she said the next day in school?

"I lost your pencil, and I am *so* sorry."

"That's okay," I said, "Just give me sixty cents to replace it."

She happily gave me the money the next day and I learned quickly about *collateral* lending to protect an investment. From that day on, anyone who wanted to use a pencil would have to give me a quarter, with my promise to return it upon his or her return of my pencil or eraser. As some of the children would take the pencils home, I began toting quarters to the mall, and learned quickly about reinvestment.

At collection time, I got back a lot of pencils that were ugly, eraser-less, and faint in scent. So I sold those pencils for fifty cents and told my new customers that if they wanted to use the pencils they would now have to buy it at sixty cents; no other deals on my desk table.

Mind you, the pencils cost about fifteen cents. But with so many selling points business was good! The use of these pencils brought even the most reclusive child an immediate elevation on the social scale. Many were more than willing to pay the price for such fame on the playground. That was priceless—even if it meant going without lunch.

During quiet time in class after the long lunch period, I would daydream about hearing pencil sharpeners whizzing all over the school as a result of all the new pencils I would sell. Word of mouth proved once again to be the strongest form of advertisement, as children from other classes placed orders for pencils and erasers.

Well not even three weeks later, my business was good and growing at a fast rate. It was a *bona fide* success! I sat there basking in glory with wadded-up dollar bills and loose change all over my desk. I slowly leaned back in my chair during the post-recess nap time, taking in my surroundings and classmates resting with their heads on their desk.

My daydream of palm fronds blowing in the gentle breeze and sunny seashores adjoining my millionaire estate was disturbed by my concerned teacher standing over my desk. She was blocking my sunlit tropical vision. She was also one of our neighbors living just a few doors from our house.

As she gently leaned over my desk and began gathering up my profits and working capital, she pleaded with me with concern and whispered caution: "You need to put this away because it won't be the pencils and erasers they will come after you for."

The very threat of affliction was poised to reveal what it was that I valued the most.

Hmm, let me think about this for a moment…

I had never considered the threat of my personal safety from the playground bully. I had *more* than lunch money at this point and I would be a prime target for her! The reality was that now that my older sister was attending junior high school at another campus and that made my back a little too drafty for me to confidently continue in this very lucrative business.

As the school day ended, my teacher gave me back my profits and working capital, which she had safely stored in her desk drawer, and I settled up with all of my customers and ended my venture.

I started off having fun as I watched the money roll in and ended up with something profound. I stumbled upon my gift to relate to people not so much from a sales perspective but empathetically. I was genuinely happy to be a part of their happiness! Though the following was intended for a different audience, there are some principles in it that are still timely for today. For one, embrace your strong will, but make choices that reflect what God values and don't let go.

> See, I set before you today life and prosperity, death and destruction. For I command you today to love the LORD your God, to walk in his ways, and to keep his commands, decrees and laws; then you

will live and increase, and the LORD your God will bless you in the land you are entering to possess. But if your heart turns away and you are not obedient, and if you are drawn away to bow down to other gods and worship them, I declare to you this day that you will certainly be destroyed. You will not live long in the land you are crossing the Jordan to enter and possess. This day I call heaven and earth as witnesses against you that I have set before you life and death, blessings and curses. Now choose life, so that you and your children may live and that you may love the LORD your God, listen to his voice, and hold fast to him. For the LORD is your life, and he will give you many years in the land he swore to give to your fathers, Abraham, Isaac and Jacob.
Deuteronomy 30:15-20 (NIV)

Queen for a Day

"You're such a saint, Janeen!"

"You have been such a courageous martyr!"

"You know…we got together and made this crown, scepter, and robe of many colors just for you. Our She-Ro!"

Boy was this coronation wonderful! Ah, to be lifted to such heights and lofty places in front of men; but, oh the depths of the fall to come.

During the turmoil in my marriage, for the few that were close enough to see what I was going through (to the extent that they could see) I gave a good number of them the power to crown me. I was after anything to soothe my hurt and pain, including power and control—real or imagined. That is what I wanted—a solution to all my problems that came from the *outside* without ever having considered the need to look *inside*.

When I allow people to lift me up, it is only a matter of time before they will let me down. I will fall because when I let others lift me up, it creates a situation in which I will forever feel indebted to them for the "lift." The fatigue of never measuring up to their whims alone will cause me to fall. Or I will fall because they can arbitrarily exercise the power they hold and snatch the pedestal from underneath me, seeing as they are the ones lifting me.

I knew that the fall was inevitable, but I stashed that thought way in the back of my mind. The "lift" is what I wanted, and I gravitated towards anything that reinforced it. I wanted to sway in the wind like the fronds of a palm tree high up in the sky, close to the sun. Of course, I was a bramble, but I allowed my fair-weather comrades to make me think my leafless skinny twigs were palm fronds. Silly, isn't it?

When I was a young adult, my pastor provided an illustration to make a point about time. He had a small sand-timer and flipped it upside down and the congregation sat and watched the sand trickle down into the lower bulb. It felt like we were in *time out*. It was only a one-minute timer but it was the longest, most boring minute I've ever spent. And I thought this sermon illustration was a waste too, until about thirty seconds into it, my mind started to wonder and reflect. He concluded and asked us how well we steward our time and then reminded us that time is precious and once it is spent, we can't get it back. It provoked even deeper thought. Good point, pastor!

Affliction does provide opportunity to consider and reflect upon what is being revealed. Jonah was in the belly of the fish for three days and three nights. That is a long time to be alone with your thoughts; to be placed on *pause*. My marital turmoil was my *pause* button but I couldn't hear the soft pleading of the Lord to accept His help until I began journaling. It was the time and moment that I needed to openly *confront* and *consider* my situation, in the light of His love for me.

I acknowledged my sinful, pride-hungry nature and dragged it under subjection to the rule of His Spirit living on the inside of me.

> This is the verdict: Light has come into the world, but men loved darkness instead of light because their deeds were evil. Everyone who does evil hates the light, and will not come into the light for fear that his deeds will be exposed. But whoever lives by the truth comes into the light, so that it may be seen plainly that what he has done has been done through God.
>
> John 3:19-21 (NIV)

Our flesh predisposes us to not see the light. Our flesh also predisposes us to desire a high place. At certain times, the temptation is greater than at others. Nonetheless, in order to not fall into a dark realm, we have to remain on our face before the Father to keep His perspective and values in clear view.

Isn't it something how so often it seems to be such little things that make great men fall?

> "Pride goes before destruction, a haughty spirit before a fall" (Proverbs 16:18, NIV).

Well P-R-I-D-E is only five letters, but it is no little thing!

I have allowed people to lift me and I have also participated in giving a "lift" to another person a time or two.

I was willing to participate in and believe I was a martyr in my marriage while adamantly overlooking that there were two sides to my story. The years of enabling him by embracing fear did help create the unhealthy environment along with other sin ish-yous I had.

Those who were rallying to "lift" me were all too willing to spoon-feed me my poisonous "me-the-martyr" version of events. But in time they got tired of holding me up with that lie. I became an arrogant victim.

As the reality of the responsibilities of caring for three children and the toll of grieving began weighing on me heavily, I got too heavy and they kicked the pedestal from underneath me and confiscated the crown, scepter, and robe they had bestowed upon me.

The choices made about how play to handle the hardballs that life threw my way were mine alone to make. It doesn't matter who was pushing or pulling me or shouting at me to "swing that bat," because ultimately I played the pitches according to what was in my own heart.

Sometimes I consulted with God, sometimes I didn't. Sometimes I played the godly pitches, and sometimes I let them pass. I am responsible for my own choices.

There was never a time when I was unable to choose which of the pitches I took or let pass. It is tempting to say that God brought hard times my way. He didn't bring them my way but He did allow them.

> "If any of you lacks wisdom, he should ask God, who gives generously to all without finding fault, and it will be given to him" (James 1:5, NIV).

One of the many blessings of being a child of the true God is that you don't have to do anything but follow Him. I can ask Him what pitch to take and wait for Him to answer. It is hard, especially in today's times to practice patience and wait but at times waiting is what is required.

Yes, Christmas is the most wonderful time of the year. Jesus was born!

> "And this shall be a sign unto you; Ye shall find the babe wrapped in swaddling clothes, lying in a manger" (Luke 2:12, KJV).

God afflicted Himself and cracked Himself open for us.

> Who, being in very nature God, did not consider equality with God something to be grasped, but made himself nothing, taking the very nature of a servant, being made in human likeness. And being found in appearance as a man, he

humbled himself and became obedient to death—even death on a cross!
Philippians 2:6-8 (NIV)

Our sinful hands helped:

> "And it was the third hour, and they crucified him" (Mark 15:25, KJV).

And now we have the greatest gift before us; an opportunity for a close relationship with the God of the universe, if we choose.

> "God did this so that they would seek him and perhaps reach out for him and find him, though he is not far from any one of us" (Acts 17:27, NIV).

He loves me and you and *whosoever* will come to Him.

> "For God so loved the world, that he gave his only begotten Son, that whosoever believeth in him should not perish, but have everlasting life" (John 3:16, KJV).

Won't you let Him love you?
Hmm, let me think about this for a moment. Yes!

It's the *little* things that often cause the greatest impact, like the babe in the manger that we acknowledge during Christmastime. In the story of Jonah, big, theatrical displays were taking place! It wasn't the great wind (1:4), the sea miraculously ceasing from raging (1:15), the great fish swallowing Jonah for three days and nights (1:17), the fish vomiting Jonah upon dry land (2:10), the barbarians having faith in God (3:5), the great gourd tree God provided to shade Jonah in the desert, but did you notice the *little* female scarlet worm (4:7). It packed a mighty punch; it helped create the environment that made Jonah suicidal.

When affliction hits, God has our attention and if we would but listen and quiet our hearts before Him, we would hear His voice through all of the turmoil and theatrical distractions that would seek to steal our focus away from Him.

The Spirit of God, His voice, is that little thing that causes the greatest impact toward turning our lives around for good if we respond yes and obey His call to us. Not that His voice is a little thing in a downgraded sense, but if you haven't honed the discipline of obeying Gods call, the craziness of life can cause it to be drowned out. But it is our ability to hear His still small voice as we are pondering our state of affliction which is critical to our ability to sense and know God's love.

In Henry Morris' book titled *Biblical Basis for Modern Science*, he provides insight about that little consequential thing to Jonah's story: the scarlet worm.

> When the female of the scarlet worm species was ready to give birth to her young, she would attach her body to the trunk of a tree, fixing herself so firmly and permanently that she would never leave again. The eggs deposited beneath her body were thus protected until the larvae were hatched and able to enter their own life cycle. As the mother died, the crimson

fluid stained her body and the surrounding wood. From the dead bodies of such female scarlet worms, the commercial scarlet dyes of antiquity were extracted. What a picture this gives of Christ, dying on the tree, shedding his precious blood that he might 'bring many sons unto glory' (Hebrews 2:10)! He died for us, that we might live through him!

The obedient sacrifice of love! Thank you Jesus!

Chapter Six

Spit Up Ashore

"And the LORD spake unto the fish, and it vomited out Jonah upon the dry land."
                              Jonah 2:10 (KJV)

I wonder how Jonah looked after being ejected by the fish. It is logical to conclude that He was covered in vomit. Yuck! I wonder if others saw him on the shore and silently stared at him in great anticipation of what he was going to do next. Or, maybe if others saw him they ran away crying, "Ugh!"

What happens after we spend time with the Lord and it changes our orientation? Does it provoke a response from the people closest to you? Should it?

My condition was altered because I had been enveloped by the Lord; we were *close*!

<u>Holy Roller</u>

So, what does that word *sanctification* mean? I thought sanctification meant to be "old and mean in the name of

Jesus." As a child, I can remember a group of elderly people in my church that referred to themselves as being "sanctified." They seemed to take great pride in that distinction, to the point of shaming and even shooing the "little lesser ones" from their presence because they had not "arrived yet" to their level of Christian achievement and righteousness.

They were "clean" and all others were "dirty". They sat up "front" and we were to keep in the "back." I decided that I *never* wanted to have the title of "sanctified" because I didn't want to ever be old and sour (not to mention *sorely unfashionable*). It also seemed too hard to ever attain. Besides, I wanted to be expressive and what they called sanctification looked like bondage!

I understand now that sanctification means to be set apart by God, for God. Though it is progressive over our lifetime, I was aware now that as a result of being near the Lord, His transformative power was making me over. Before, void of this progressively deepening understanding of God's love, I was missing out on the confidence, courage, and empowerment that comes with knowing that you are *close* with the almighty God. I would miss out no longer!

> "If a man cleanses himself from the latter he will be an instrument for noble purposes, made holy, useful to the Master and prepared to do any good work" (2 Timothy 2:21, NIV).

> "But you are a chosen people, a royal priesthood, a holy nation, a people belonging to God, that you may declare

the praises of him who called you out of
darkness into his wonderful light"
1 Peter 2:9 (NIV)

Now that the hemorrhaging stopped and the healing was progressing, I needed to begin walking and demonstrating my faith in God, like physical therapy that helps recover and return your strength. Time to remember and demonstrate what I know!

"When my life was ebbing away, I remembered you, Lord, and my prayer rose to you, to your holy temple" (Jonah 2:7, NIV).

Jonah had a lot of time to think: three days and three nights in the belly of the fish. His plight brings to mind the story of the prodigal son in Luke 15. He too found himself lost in the *life crazies* and it landed him in a place that provided afflicting conditions and a moment to think his predicament over.

Thank God we were moving further away from *that place* and closer to home. I began increasing in strength one step at a time. Just when I thought my legs would give out, a breakthrough propelled me forward as I remembered how Christ walked.

Imitate Christ

"Fake it 'til you make it" is probably the worst advice floating around out there today. I am not certain whom to credit for this gem of pop psychology.

Better counsel is to prepare for the season you hope for. Don't fake it, pretending that the season already exists. That is presumption and presumption is *not* faith. Faith is what pleases God. Presumption is as foolish as wearing a full-length mink coat to lunch in August in sunny southern California as if it were winter in New England. It is sorely out of order and hurtful, consistently leaving you disappointed and discouraged from unmet expectations.

I remember practicing gymnastics for hours at a club that produced an Olympic athlete. There is an uneven bars combination skill called a "glide kip." A glide is when you simply hold onto the bar and swing your suspended body in a fluid forward motion. A kip is when you pull your body up atop the bar, in one motion, as you begin the swing backwards out of the glide move.

"Steve," as I shall refer to him, was one of my coaches at the Charter Oak Gymnastics Club, and on this particular evening, I was practicing like a mad woman trying to get that skill. Steve came over and tried to show me that getting this skill combination was kind of like pulling up a pair of pants while getting dressed. Easy for him to say! I was so frustrated that I couldn't get it. He made it sound so simple!

I tried to tell myself that it was only hard because I was attempting it in a pike position rather than a straddled one. But that wasn't why (for those of you not familiar with gymnastics, bear with me for just a moment). The problem was that my technique was wrong.

I don't know whether it was sweat or tears in my eyes, but all I could see was red!

Steve yelled over to me and said, "Janeen, it's just like pulling up a pair of pants."

I tried hard to imagine that as I attempted the combination over and over again. The palms of my hands were shredded to bits from the friction of the uneven bars. Chalk was all over me. Steve could tell I was exhausted because he teased me a little at the break in my form as I began to kick and wiggle in a desperate attempt to get my hips on top of that bar.

Anyway, Steve walked over and told me to go get some water. I didn't want to. I wanted to get that skill. But he insisted that I immediately stop and get a drink of water. That made me even madder!

"Practice makes perfect," I told him, my tone sharp, "and I gotta practice to get this now!" Then he said something to me that has proven such a valuable nugget of wisdom. "Janeen," he said, "practice makes *habits*. If you practice it wrong, it will take more time to learn it the right way."

That was the best drink of cold water I had ever had, and I got the skill down before I left that night. I apply that nugget of wisdom in my pursuit of being Christ-like. Practice makes habits—not perfection. Imitating Christ could not be accomplished by my doing what I thought was right or what I thought it looked like, but only by accepting and obeying instruction on what was the correct way. This process is lifelong, but it is not a blind undertaking. I have the Father who tells me how, Christ who has shown me, and the Spirit who helps me do it.

> "Whoever claims to live in him must walk as Jesus did" (1 John 2:6-7, NIV).

> "Therefore be imitators of God, as beloved children…" (Ephesians 5:1, NASB).

One step at a time, keep walking and you will continue growing in strength and you will be transformed. Demonstrate your faith in Him by trusting that He knows what you need and will take care of you.

Trust God? Trust God!

When I was in college before I married, I worked, lived in my own apartment, and paid my own bills. I was leading a relatively responsible young adult life. Things were much different for me after I married and had children. My husband and I agreed on the importance of my staying home with the children, at least until they began school. Financially it also made sense, seeing that most of the money I would have earned at the time would have gone to childcare expenses.

On the surface, it all looked so good, but underneath was a neglectful shame. I remember a church member seeing a huge blown-out hole in my pantyhose that my suit skirt couldn't cover up when I was seated. Once, a minister's wife scolded me about the need for me to brush my daughter's "nappy hair." She didn't know and probably wouldn't have believed that I did not have a brush for her soft hair, so I had been wetting and gathering it into a pigtail to the best of my ability. They just couldn't imagine that I had no financial resources to purchase the needed pair of panty hose or a hairbrush.

His neglect of the children and me led to more daily drama and stress than I care to recall. This behavior was magnified with children.

While I was working my fanny off as a homemaker, I constantly felt as though I had to approach him with my needs apologetically because I did not have any income.

There was plenty of money coming into the house, but he often reminded me by his words and, more often, by his behavior that it was not my money.

His greatest leverage over me was that I lacked my own access to and control of finances. It had always been effective in keeping me "in line" and "under control." Neglect was a powerful weapon used on me to make me feel as though I had no rights and no voice to ask for what the children or I needed.

I was so often deprived of the most basic practical needs that I felt as though I had nothing. I tried to earn money through entrepreneurial ventures but to no avail. He would often have last-minute changes of heart that forced me to take the children with me to board meetings of the non-profit I founded. I had even taken them with me to clean the house of a wealthy family that I worked for.

I had no real viable options for working outside the home because there weren't any positions that would allow me to take the children with me.

Well, although I was the same dress size for years, fashion styles had definitely changed. I decided that I would let go and reduce my wardrobe. I read Anne Ortlund's book *Disciplines of a Beautiful Woman,* which helped me understand stewardship with clothing in a whole new light. I followed her advice and got rid of garments that were torn, faded, worn, or outdated—or all of the above. I mean, come on, is it really appropriate to wear a faded taffeta prom dress to run errands?

This effort was going to reduce my wardrobe to slim pickings, but I needed to admit that I needed new clothing.

He always committed to making me look like the toast of the town on Sunday morning for church service, but when the clock struck midnight on Monday morning the gown, slippers, and stagecoach turned back. I had been so used to looking in a closet full of nothing to wear that the thought of not having to stress out doing that anymore was a welcome change.

The benefit of reducing my wardrobe as a matter of practical sense was liberating—it freed me from stress and wasted time. The stress came largely from *his* response to my utterance of the old line: "I have nothing to wear." "Woman," he would say, "you got a whole closet full of clothes. Surely, there is something in there for you to wear."

It was a little scary at first because the children were growing like weeds and I did need presentable clothing for running errands in the community. I dared to trust that God was concerned about what concerned me when it came to my food, clothing, and shelter needs.

> "…for your heavenly Father knows that you need all these things" (Matthew 6:32b, NASB).

I had felt uncomfortable walking around looking less than my best for far too long.

Maternity clothes, layettes, baby blankets, bottles, monitors, and toys were surrendered. Plastic pumps from the 80s, Sunday hats with bent rims or felt rubbed thin beyond repair were offered up. No item was too sacred to be hauled off to the local thrift store or out to the trash. By the bagful, junk got the boot!

I giggled a lot during the three days it took to complete this thinning task. In spite of the protest and promises that I would "regret it," I trusted God to provide what the children and I needed. I started to demonstrate my belief that God was trustworthy and would faithfully grant requests for the legitimate physical needs of His children.

After I completed the task, I lay prostrate in prayer to God, not knowing what to say. I was thankful but concerned, trusting but insecure. Guess what? The very next morning I received a huge bag of clothes that were not only stylish but *fit* me. Two days later there came another huge bag of clothes that were not only stylish but fit the *children*. God used a very special lady, who was struggling through her own marital turmoil, to bless me and my babies.

Who would have imagined that she, too, would feel inclined to do some cleaning of her own and give the items to me? She and I were the same size. She also had children who were growing like weeds so I had "choice pickings" for my own. She had *no* idea what was going on behind our closed doors, but God did all along.

In the wake of this unmistakable display of God's power to reward openly those who seek Him in secret, I drew closer to Him in confident trust. It encouraged me to continue demonstrating my faith in God. I was beginning to transform.

'Bout Time

Well there I sat on the floor of our family room, exhausted from the rigors of the day as a homemaker and mom of three toddlers, now ages two, three, and four years old. I was bursting with a sense of excitement that I could not quite explain. It was as if a cool breeze had blown across my hot face and managed to clear away a veil of dimness in my eyes.

The pinhole of light that shined through at the hospital two years before had become a beam growing inside me. The breach in the dam was bigger now and the sound of the pressure being let off was louder and the flow greater as it washed up the debris.

The house had been looking like a fortified demonic stronghold pretty consistently over the years, especially in the kitchen and laundry departments. I could not remember the last time there had been a drawer full of clean silverware or a dresser full of clean underwear. There were more Sundays he stood before the congregation delivering the sermon in swim trunks underneath his dry-cleaned designer suit than I would care to recall.

But this day, as I sat there on the floor of the family room, I was so tired of the mess that I was determined that my home would be in this shape *no longer!* I made a decision.

It was about 8:30 p.m. and I began cleaning the house from top to bottom with zest and zeal. An unmistakable newness was looming in the air (not just from the air freshener's fresh clean scent). It was strange.

After determining in my heart to get this menial task completed, I could almost touch this presence enveloping me with an endearing affirmation as I steadily worked along from one room of the house to the next. My energy level and passion to get it all done was positively supernatural! I cleaned the house from top to bottom before, but this time it was somehow markedly different.

Between each completed sink full of washed dishes, I would throw another load of dirty clothes in the washer, and throw out a moldy pile (as a result of excess laundry being thrown onto the basement floor, which frequently flooded), then fold up what was left of the freshly cleaned ones.

Instead of vacuuming the carpeted two-story parsonage we called home, I swept the floors with a broom so as not to awaken everyone in the house.

I finally finished the cleaning at about 3:00 a.m. It was all picked up, spic and span. Even though I knew my youngest child would be awakening shortly and the day would dawn and tap what little energy I had left, I felt rested and energized. Free! I felt like throwing a party. So I did the unthinkable. I threw Luther Vandross on the CD player and swayed to the music. It was wonderful.

While there were well over 300 gospel CDs and about twenty secular CDs in our house, I had not selected and played a CD in our home for years! Something so simple had eluded me all of this time and a tear trickled down my cheek as I realized it. It also dawned on me that I had not opened the mail or answered the phone or the door in a long time either. This moment was rich beyond description.

Instantly, layers of bondage that had barred me from such basic personal freedoms fell away and renewed courage took its place. A part of me came back to life, that for all intents and purposes was *dead*. I had become aware, much like a baby who is entertained by the sound of her very own giggle. Suddenly and oddly, I got tickled silly, too.

Just as I was drifting down memory lane with Luther Vandross' greatest hits, I heard a jarring *buzz*! I had forgotten all about that last load of clothes in the dryer. But I tell you that though the dryer signal startled me, the sounds of liberty's bells rang out over it. As a matter of fact, as I was nearing the end of folding that last load of laundry, that bell was ringing so loudly it awakened him!

As the door to the den flung open, the gale force wind of negative emotions and bitter words were stirred against my back once again. This time I wasn't afraid. I ignored him for the first time in years. He eventually just walked out, still fussing and fuming but walked out nonetheless.

That first-grade, hide-and-seek champion was peeking out from behind the wall, demonstrating confident trust in God's love, care, and His protection. I was being transformed.

Shopping For The Free Indeed

Well, the heart of that first-grade champion was reviving more and more each day. For starters, I wasn't playing anymore and the remnants of hiding places were coming down, beginning with the parsonage walls…or at least the drawbridge over the moat. I was leaving the driveway! To the grocery store! Unaccompanied!

In preparation for my *grand junk food acquisition*, I had to pull out an old checkbook of mine to study it. I had worked at a bank before, but it had been so long since I had written a check, or even seen one, that I had forgotten how to fill one out. It had been so long, in fact, that I wondered if my account had been subjected to escheatment.

I called the bank to get a status on my account and confirmed I had about eight dollars.

At the store, I took my time selecting my items. I got a candy bar, bag of chips, and bottle of soda. But what I remember most was the near debilitating feelings of insecurity I had at the checkout counter. When it was time to write the check to pay for my items, I felt so sick. I was visibly nervous because I had become so conditioned by the years of extreme manipulation. Money for a trip to the beauty parlor taken away minutes before my scheduled appointment to teach me a "lesson," keys to the car and house secretly removed from my key chain to leverage his demand for his terms to be met. All that made this simple transaction at the grocery store a bondage breaker. It was a tough nut to crack!

I was so fidgety that the cashier called the manager over for verification of the check, which made me even more fidgety. The check was only a little over three dollars! I wanted to run, but I prayerfully fought the urge and planted myself in my resolve to stand. The following verse echoed from the night before:

> For God did not give us a spirit of timidity (of cowardice, of craven and cringing and fawning fear), but [He has given us a spirit] of power and of love and of calm *and* well-balanced mind *and* discipline *and* self-control.
> 2 Timothy 1:7 (AMPC)

I had successfully made the purchase and I couldn't help but giggle as I reclined in the car and took a bite from my candy bar and saddled up for the ride home. It was a trip!

I was near manic as I constantly checked and readjusted my mirrors to ensure that I wasn't displeasing any drivers around me with my speed or lane choice.

I passed the turn onto the street where I lived twice! The first time was because I didn't want to anger the car approaching in my turn lane. I really didn't want any confrontation with him by making him think I was "cutting him off" at the pass by moving into *his* lane too abruptly. So I did not exercise my right and allow myself to choose to signal and change lanes. Instead, I let his convenience take precedence over my incredible *inconvenience*.

The second time was when I nearly caused an accident trying desperately to avoid a confrontation with another driver. He was pulling his way out of a side street illegally, and I held up traffic at the major intersection to assist him, which succeeded in making everyone behind me very mad at me!

In my effort to lag far enough behind to avoid all those drivers I had upset, I sped past my street for the second time.

I drove down a half a mile and took refuge in a library parking lot for about ten minutes and thought about what had just happened. Those other drivers clearly disagreed with my commitment to sacrifice my self-will for another. My avoidance of confrontation was dangerous to me and to them. That conditioned mindset was on its way out, forever!

Well, I finally arrived home safely, though I was clearly shaken. I dragged all of my strewed emotions in the door and quietly settled my body in the chair at the table.

Victory.

As I sat there sipping my soda and chomping on my chips, I began to reflect and examine my heart about the events of the day, which started before I jumped in the "getaway" car.

I had answered the phone before I left for the store, and amidst the major conflict that action stirring up, I intercepted the mail and sorted it while asking him direct questions about some of the contents. This was no easy task considering that at some point in my spiritual development I was poisoned by toxic theology—which is sort of like bad seafood—especially with the misinterpretation of the following verse: "Do nothing out of selfish ambition or vain conceit, but in humility consider others better than yourselves" (Philippians 2:3, NIV).

As I sat there at the table finishing up my junk food feast, I quietly pondered my marriage. Though my heart's will was getting stronger it needed a heavy dose of Godly boundaries and "tough love." I needed to separate from him, but all those years during which my self-worth eroded left me afraid to make the change.

My fear was bigger than the God I claimed to believe in! Though I knew He created the world, I made decisions as though He was incapable of caring for the material needs of my children and me. Intellectually, I knew the facts about the marvelous exploits performed by the God of Bible I professed to believe in, but my low self-worth impeded the Bible's ability to become practical revelation in my life. That conditioned mindset was on its way out, forever as I continued to demonstrate my faith in God and allow its transformative power to prevail.

Sin-Explainer

As I've shared this book and testimony with others, there was a common recurring theme with many that shared their stories and testimonies with me: they were enablers. In short, they would *not* call sin, sin, especially when it came to their closest relationships with others.

There was a common tendency to try to rationalize sin or explain it away as something other than sin. As a result, they were left trying to cope with a sinful situation and prolonged securing a real resolution to their relational problems. Hope is necessary and powerful but you can't cope with sin in hopes that it will get better, sin must be shut down and forsaken.

I'd previously become a *sin-explainer* and normalized this behavior to cope. This coping tool got me nothing but tangled in the net of a spiritually heretical and emotionally toxic belief system. This belief system cruelly entangled me further and would not agree to let me go, no matter how hard I tried to reason with it; exposure to lingering sin can severely infect right thinking.

I was so thankful that God never let me go and kept His promise to love me in spite of me. I couldn't help but feel like Jonah when he said;

> "But I, with a song of thanksgiving, will sacrifice to you. What I have vowed I will make good. I will say, 'Salvation comes from the LORD'" (Jonah 2:9, NIV).

The more I demonstrated my faith in God, the more I transformed. I began using my voice. I had been yelled at and told, "Shut up, you can't sing anyway" and had not sung in years, but God's spirit was living in my heart and feared no man.

> "The LORD is my light and my salvation; whom shall I fear? the LORD is the strength of my life; of whom shall I be afraid?" (Psalm 27:1, KJV).

I started to sing again and I even wrote my first song, "God Sees."

> "God sees He knows beneath that smile you hide behind
> God sees He knows beneath those dreams you're afraid to live
> The eye of the Master Divine sees you there

JOURNEY TO LOVE

Come out come out from hiding He sees you there
He awaits your hand to take your cares
He's strong enough to bear the weight of all your burdens
His loving eyes they see you and care
The eye of the Master Divine sees you there

God sees He knows beneath that pain you've held within
God sees He knows beneath that hurt you've denied its cry
The eye of the Master Divine sees you there

The God I serve He's waiting there beside you
He'll lift your head when skies are grey
When burdened down He'll lift the weight off of your shoulders
His loving eyes they see you and care
The eye of the Master Divine sees you there

God sees He knows beneath the joy replaced by fear
God sees He knows behind that masquerading calm
The eye of the Master Divine sees you there

Don't hide cry out to God then let it go you'll only grow
Just remember this one thing this one thing oh

God sees and He knows beneath that
pain you've held within
God sees He knows beneath that hurt
you've denied its cry
The eye of the Master Divine sees you there
The eye of the Master Divine sees you there
The Master He sees you and He cares

He sees you there, He sees you there
And I know He cares
He sees you there, He sees you there
And I know He cares"
(BMI, copyright 2002)

Every time that we demonstrate our faith in God, we draw closesr to Him and He proves Himself faithful to us. Through the enablement of the Holy Spirit, I was being transformed and am so grateful to God!

I was so grateful but wondered how I could ever repay the kindness and patience God had shown me, not to mention His immense love for me. What do you give to someone who already has everything? You!

Chapter Seven

Heart and Song of the Matter

> *"So the people of Nineveh believed God, and proclaimed a fast, and put on sackcloth, from the greatest of them even to the least of them."*
>
> Jonah 3:5 (KJV)

Beginning to demonstrate my belief in God by walking according to His promises and character was transformative, one step at a time. But the relational closeness that God and I desired was not achieved on account me *doing* right but rather by my *being* right; the heart of the matter for us is having an upright heart before God.

> "Create in me a pure heart, O God, and renew a steadfast spirit within me" (Psalm 51:10, NIV).

> The men of Nineveh will stand up at the judgment with this generation and condemn it; for they repented at the preach-

ing of Jonah, and now something greater than Jonah is here.
Matthew 12:41 (NIV)

The people of Nineveh repented. Their actions detailed in Jonah 3 (fasting, putting on sackcloth, sitting in ashes, etc.) was an outward expression of an inward change. They got to the heart of the matter: reverent submission.

> My sacrifice [the sacrifice acceptable] to God is a broken spirit; a broken and a contrite heart [broken down with sorrow for sin and humbly and thoroughly penitent], such, O God, You will not despise.
> Psalm 51:17 (AMPC)

There is no record that Jonah told them *how* to repent, *encouraged* them to repent, or that there would even be hope for them *if* they did repent. The Bible records Jonah as only saying one simple and true thing to the people of Nineveh:

> "…Yet forty days, and Nineveh shall be overthrown" (Jonah 3:4b, KJV).

But they did repent! What prompted them to do such a thing? Being visited by a simple and true Word from heaven!

Soul Pouring

For me "*soul pouring*," as I called it, was a movement in my childhood church's Sunday worship service that scared the devil out of me. This movement was actually called the "altar call."

The *soul pouring* began when one of the church's deacons would lead the congregation in the joint reading of a simple Bible passage like the Twenty-Third Psalm. After the passage was read, he and the other deacons standing at the front of the church would then turn around and kneel on the altar which looked like a long carpet covered park bench. The congregants were invited to join them around the altar. And then would begin what I thought was a frightening incantation to summon the spirits from beyond and awaken the dead!

Some of these good folks to include members of my family would be moaning, praying, crying, shouting out loud and singing, all at the same time.

During this time, there was one song they always sang in response to the reading of God's Word, that nailed my fear on the head and my fanny to the pew or, when I was younger, to my mama's lap. It was a hymn written circa 1719 by Isaac Watts titled, "I Love The Lord."

Long Meter or *Dr. Watts* was a reference for a compilation of hymns in the old African American Church that were comprised of lyrics only without musical notation. As a result the musical arrangement slightly varied from congregation to congregation, but the core melodic structure was the same as well as the format. As far as format, it was *call and response*, meaning that one person would lead the selection by first calling out a verse and cuing the congregants to respond back in kind.

For this particular call and response song, it would start out with the deacon speedily and melodically calling out the lyrics, "I Love the Lord, He heard my cry," immediately followed by the congregation's response, repeating the same lyric in a slow, deeply thoughtful and spiritual arrangement. Without fail, before the leading deacon finished that very first line, people would start shouting, screaming, wailing, and crying aloud all over the sanctuary!

Granted, other mines of demonstrative expression typically detonated throughout the service such as when the tenor section sang their chorus part alone followed by the sopranos' hitting the high note and the pastor beginning to whoop but nothing like this moment; the *soul pouring*.

My goal each and every Sunday morning was not to be around during the *soul pouring*. I'd go so far as to even try to cause my family to be too late to get there in time for it, since it always occurred near the beginning of service, before the choir marched in. That *soul pouring* worship activity left me undone every time. It was wild!

I was just a little girl and didn't have too much theology, but I could *feel!* This *soul pouring* movement seemed to always usher in the presence of the very living God, and it was His presence that scared me to death because it was so overwhelmingly awesome. I was not used to such an emotional tugging on my heart and just by being in His presence, whether I was participating in the *soul pouring* or not, yanked on my heart strings.

His presence is truly awesome!

My feeling of being overwhelmed during the *soul pouring* was enhanced by the depth of the effect His presence had on those who were participating in the *soul pouring*. As they cried out to the Lord, it was as if all of their hopes, dreams, ish-yous, oppressions, hurts, dismays, and disappointments poured out in an almost theatrical setting like a blood sacrifice described in the Old Testament or like this picture we are given of the Ninevites in Jonah 3.

I could almost feel their faith in God's capacity to love them through it all as they soaked up His presence. As I mentioned earlier, my family was not the "touchy-feely" kind, but there was something about the manifest presence of God that provided an "exhale" for burdens that a mask couldn't stand in the presence of. Even Mrs. Malone didn't look as mean! (I'll get to *her* in a moment).

Being visited by a simple and true Word from heaven moved upon our hearts. Our response in song with unashamed hope, merciful pleas, and shouts of thankfulness to God that He would take the time to *stop by* was overwhelmingly disarming. Pretense could not comfortably stand in the presence of it. And so it is as we demonstrate our faith in God, it flows from the heart and not a systematic, routine checklist.

> For the word of God is quick, and powerful, and sharper than any two-edged sword, piercing even to the dividing asunder of soul and spirit, and of the joints and marrow, and is a discerner of the thoughts and intents of the heart.
> Hebrews 4:12 (KJV)

Whether standing, sitting, or laying in His presence during the hearing of God's Word and responding from the heart was a critical lifeline for those participants. I could not understand it as a child, but I certainly could feel it, and at this point in my life, *soul pouring* is a critical lifeline for me. It's the heart of the matter; the spiritual discipline of sacrificial worship.

Just to be clear, *soul pouring* is not some strange fire. It is simply an expression of the hope of God's intervention, through a lamentation, as indicated by the inspiration of the lyricist Dr. Isaac Watts:

> In 1714, Queen Anne of England lay dying, and she had no son or daughter to succeed her. Who would be the new ruler? All of Britain was concerned.
>
> Isaac Watts had reason to worry. His father had been imprisoned under the previous regime because his views did not please the ruling family. As a young child, Isaac had been carried by his mother to visit his father in jail. Queen Anne had brought a new tolerance and had given freedom to Isaac's father.

These remarks are attributed to his hymn, "O God, Our Help In Ages Past" but clearly also reflects that deeply personal story of Dr. Watts in his song, "I Love The Lord."

> "I love you, Lord; you heard my cries,
> and pitied every groan;
> Long as I live, when troubles rise,
> I'll hasten to your throne.
>
> I love you, Lord; you bow your ear;
> you're ever good and just.
> Then let my heart feel no despair!
> Your power has all my trust.
>
> If you behold me sore distressed,
> you bid my pains remove;

> I'll turn my soul to you, my rest,
> and witness to your love."

No giant multimedia screens, no band, no accompaniment tracks, no world-renowned musician, soloist, choir, group, or clinician could teach me what this time of worship did for me.

There is something unmistakably powerful about being visited by a simple and true Word from heaven.

Let's recap a summary outline of how journeying with the Lord happens.

First, God initiates and calls us to Himself.

Second, God calls a time out, using whatever means that will get our attention. It may be His simple and true words, affliction, a miracle that He performs, turmoil in our marriage, the fury or breathtaking beauty of nature, or whatever He chooses.

Third, God reveals His commitment to be with us always.

Fourth, we are given opportunity to respond to God.

God's Words are loaded with mercy, whether or not they are explained or expounded upon well. God's Words explain themselves best. Even when His Words are commandments, all of His words are for our own good not just for the purpose of Him just bossing us around. He wants us to give Him our hearts so that He can take care of it.

> "Take my yoke upon you, and learn of
> me; for I am meek and lowly in heart:
> and ye shall find rest unto your souls"
> (Matthew 11:29, KJV).

Here, God sent Jonah as a means to tap the people of Nineveh on the shoulder to get their attention and give God their hearts. Also, we see God's mercy and commitment toward his creation because He gave them time to think about what He said, through Jonah. As cited in *Spurgeon's Sermon Notes*,

> I saw a cannon shot off. The men at whom it was leveled fell flat on the ground, and so escaped the bullet. Against such blows, falling is all the fencing, and prostration all the armor of proof. But that which gave them notice to fall down was their perceiving of the fire before the ordinance was discharged. Oh! The mercy of that fire, which, as it were, repenting of the mischief it had done, and the murder it might make, ran a race, and outstripped the bullet, that men (at the sight thereof) might be provided, when they could not resist to prevent it! Thus every murdering-piece is also a warning-piece against itself.
>
> God, in like manner, warns before he wounds; frights before he fights 'Yet forty days, and Nineveh shall be overthrown.' Oh, let us fall down before the Lord our Maker! Then shall his anger be pleased to make in us a daily pass-over, and his bullets leveled at us must fly above us.
>
> Thomas Fuller,
> *Spurgeon's Sermon Notes*

God doesn't desire to destroy His creation, no matter how far they've strayed.

> The Lord does not delay *and* is not tardy *or* slow about what He promises, according to some people's conception of slowness, but He is long-suffering (extraordinarily patient) toward you, not desiring that any should perish, but that all should turn to repentance.
> 2 Peter 3:9 (AMPC)

It is so critically important that we grow in our understanding of Him so that we can see His commitment being revealed to us and see the heart of the matter—His love for us.

Understanding

Reading the Bible is a spiritual discipline that is critical to our ability to relate with God. It helps us to see the intent behind what He is saying, which is always that He loves us. It enables us to see Him revealing His commitment to us, no matter the situation we find ourselves in.

I took Spanish in high school and college. My bilingual instructors could always understand me when I spoke English. The confusion and misunderstanding in our communication occurred when they spoke Spanish to me and as I feebly tried to speak Spanish back to them. Why? Spanish was not my native language; I did not know it well enough to always speak or understand it effectively as I did with English. I would have to invest my time and study Spanish. There are no shortcuts to the process of learning and growing; it takes time and commitment. Learning God's Word is critical to our relationship with God in much the same way.

If my daughter tells my son ten minutes before dinner time, "Mom said that we can have all of the chocolate chip cookies now," my son would question that. Why? Because it does not sound like *my* words or something that I would say. I would *not* tell them that they can have all of the chocolate cookies right before dinner. My son can only confidently identify error and the misrepresentation of me because of his level of relationship with me; he knows my words.

It is critical that all children know the voice of their parents. It helps them keep safe and out of needless relational insecurity and trouble. Our need to know the words of our heavenly Father is no different; it is critical lest we are deceived by the enemy and be led away from the safest place for us, or into needless trouble or relational insecurity. We've got to know the Father's words.

> "Thy word is a lamp unto my feet, and a light unto my path" (Psalm 119:105, KJV).

Being able to understand what God is saying to us requires that we study His words, the Bible. I purchased flashcards as many people do when learning a new language. In this case, the flash cards were scripture memory verse cards. The more we study His words, as written in the Holy Bible, the more clearly we hear and understand His voice when He speaks to us, as well as discern when His voice is being imitated by the enemy in effort to thwart our connection with our Maker. I grew in my understanding and communicated better with God. My prayer life matured in speech and eloquence though it is still frequently doused with hope-filled, grateful and often repentant tears.

Communicate Commitment

In addition to sacrificial worship, reading, and knowing the Word of God, prayer is a spiritual discipline that is also key to maintaining relational closeness with the Lord.

The soothing touch needed in the deepest part of the soul is met and satisfied during prayer, especially intentionally planned and consecrated prayer. I can't explain the mechanics of the *before* and *after* impact prayer has on the emotions; it's supernatural and it is transformative in the real sense. It gives peace.

> Be careful for nothing; but in everything by prayer and supplication with thanksgiving let your requests be made known unto God. And the peace of God, which passeth all understanding, shall keep your hearts and minds through Christ Jesus.
> Philippians 4:6-7 (KJV)

Prayer is simply having a conversation with God by both talking and listening. It is a holy transaction. The more I prayed the more at peace I felt.

Prayer is not a native language to people. The Creator of prayer, God, can always understand us because He created us and the very place where the prayer voice is seated—our heart. He hears us and understands us, so by *all* means, pray!

> "This is the confidence we have in approaching God: that if we ask anything according to his will, he hears us" (1 John 5:14, NIV).

God is so much more than the Great Almighty judge, although as His children, we are to respect him. I learned that there is no need to be intimidated to pray to Him. Jonah provides example that God does not give His children the silent treatment or cold shoulder. He answers yes, no, wait, and may even repeat Himself or perhaps even correct us but one thing is sure, He does not leave us to figure things out by ourselves.

God heard every prayer that Jonah offered, even while Jonah was walking out the consequences of his decision to ignore God and even when his prayers were frighteningly irreverent (Jonah 4:2-3).

It is simply not true that in order for God to hear and accept your prayer, it must be nice and neat enough, containing all of the right words and proper grammar. All that is needed is to just talk to Him from a sincere heart. This is also reflected in the recording of the Psalms.

A psalm is a poem intended to be sung; an expression of the heart to God or about God. Our communication with God should be an expression of our heart, not in the poetic sense but transparent and unfiltered, without pretense.

In his book, *Praying the Psalms, Engaging Scripture And The Life of the Spirit*, Walter Brueffemann says:

> The Psalms mostly do not emerge out of such situations of equilibrium. Rather, people are driven to such poignant prayer and song as are found in the Psalter precisely by experiences of dislocation and relocation. It is experiences of being overwhelmed, nearly destroyed, and surprisingly given life that empower us to pray and sing… This kind of speech resists

discipline, shuns precision, delights in ambiguity, is profoundly creative, and is itself an exercise in freedom.

In other words, when praying to God, let it rip! Approach God, praying with your sincerest heart as you continuously grow in your knowledge of Him. Prayer will close space between you and God much like as a child sitting in their parents' lap, laying their head on their chest and listening to their heartbeat.

Through this discipline of consecrated prayer, we grow in our understanding of Him as our good Father, our daddy God.

> "You keep track of all my sorrows. You have collected all my tears in your bottle. You have recorded each one in your book" (Psalm 56:8, NLT).

My prayer for each of us is like that of the old church hymn chorus:

> "Draw me nearer, nearer blessed Lord,
> To the cross where Thou hast died;
> Draw me nearer, nearer blessed Lord,
> To Thy precious, bleeding side."

The story of this song and its writer goes as follows:

> One evening as Fanny Crosby visited his home (William Doane, music composer) in Cincinnati, they were talking about what a wonderful thing it is to enjoy the

nearness of God, to feel his presence, to delight in his love. Suddenly Fanny Crosby, the famous blind songwriter, stopped and said she had an idea for a song. Line by line, verse by verse, she dictated it to him. The next morning, Doane added the music. Fanny Crosby found delight in writing gospel songs; William Doane found delight serving as a Christian businessman. But both agreed that there was no delight that equaled the delight of enjoying the presence of God.

The verses that accompany that chorus are so apropos:

"Consecrate me now to Thy service, Lord,
By the pow'r of grace divine;
Let my soul look up with a steadfast hope,
And my will be lost in Thine.

O the pure delight of a single hour
That before Thy throne I spend,
When I kneel in prayer, and with Thee, my God,
I commune as friend with friend!

There are depths of love that I cannot know
Till I cross the narrow sea;
There are heights of joy that I may not reach
Till I rest in peace with Thee."

Amen!

Old Mother Nurse

There were ladies at my childhood church who always wore white. From head to toe, hat to glove, stocking to shoe: white. I knew some of them as "nurses." I knew the others as "mothers." For the most part the "mothers" were older women, and they usually sat up front in their own section of the sanctuary, the "nurses" were distinguishable by the nurse caps that they wore. I had a hard time telling the mothers from the nurses apart because they were all taller than me so I called them all "Old Mother Nurses."

One in particular was very fiery! She was a little lady, short and thin, but she had a reputation among the little kids as being a real big *meanie*. I can see the face of Ms. Malone to this day. She was my childhood Sunday school teacher and one of the old mother nurses. She always seemed to sit right behind the section of pews in the back of the church where the youth sat together in silent rebellion.

The only time you wouldn't catch the youth huddled together back there was on the third Sunday, which was Youth Sunday. On that Sunday, the youth choir would sing and be gathered up in the choir loft *partying* in the name of Jesus.

There were so many traditions in my church that I absolutely thought I would never understand and always despise. One was the use of the hymnbook—ugh. I wanted to *party* as a youth choir member and as Christendom was coming into a new style of worship I thought it was only relevant if you had an overhead projector with songs that had no more than a few lines of lyrics and a cool beat. But oh no! At my church we still used hymnbooks—ugh.

Anyway, Ms. Malone was the type who would come up behind during the singing of one of the stanzas and hand you a hymnal, opened up to the right page, and point to the lyrics as they were being sung. She would insist that you sing along, almost pull your ear as a mother would do but she was also like a nurse, though, as she would administer the gross, boring hymnal medication; 'til all that "good music" was swallowed down.

Like a new tube of toothpaste, it wasn't until I was having really bad day that "It is Well with My Soul" squeezed up and out of me. After I let it pour out of me, with tears flowing, I looked around thinking, *where did that come from?*

> "When peace like a river attendeth my way,
> When sorrows like sea-billows roll;
> Whatever my lot, Thou hast taught me
> to say,
> It is well, it is well with my soul.

This hymn writer demonstrates the example of confidence in God's intentions toward us, in that they are always good and that He loves us, no matter the situation we face. As described by William J. & Ardythe Petersen in their book, *The Complete Book of Hymns.*

> The year had been filled with tragedy when Horatio Spafford, a forty-three-year-old Chicago businessman, penned this hymn. He and his wife were still grieving over the death of their son when the Great Chicago fire struck and caused them financial disaster. He realized that his family needed to get away, so that Fall he decided to take his wife and four daughters to England. His wife

and daughters went ahead on the *SS Ville du Havre*; he planned to follow in a few days.

But on the Atlantic, the *Ville du Havre* was struck by another ship and sank within twelve minutes. More than two hundred lives were lost, including the Spaffords' four daughters. When the survivors were brought to the shore at Cardiff, Wales, Mrs. Spafford cabled her husband with the words, "Saved alone."

He booked passage on the next ship. It was while crossing the Atlantic that Spafford penned the words to the hymn: "When sorrows like sea-billows roll… It is well, it is well with my soul."

As we continue to grow in our understanding of God's truth, His ways, and character, in that He so loves us, the more honest we become with ourselves. We can't help but respond to Him by giving Him ourselves and trusting Him with leading and guiding the details of our lives.

> For I am persuaded beyond doubt (am sure) that neither death nor life, nor angels nor principalities, nor things impending *and* threatening nor things to come, nor powers, Nor height nor depth, nor anything else in all creation will be able to separate us from the love of God which is in Christ Jesus our Lord.
> Romans 8:38-39 (AMPC)

Faith n' Song

> "But without faith it is impossible to please him: for he that cometh to God must believe that he is, and that he is a rewarder of them that diligently seek him." (Hebrews 11:6, KJV).

I am a worship leader (thank you Ms. Malone) and hundreds of people see me every Sunday, lifting my God high in song that people may see Him too. My ability to effectively serve God in this way is not so much a result of maintaining spiritual disciplines like a strategic checklist, but meaningfully connecting with God in my personal time and spaces from the heart.

As I shared earlier about *soul pouring*, many of the deacons that led the song could not carry a tune in a bucket but they were connected, making the worship experience authentic and powerful. I remember one elderly lady singing a song during a church service and did not hit *one* single note, but there was not a dry eye in the place. She was connected and the purity of her connection pierced our hearts as she relayed a word from heaven in song.

As worshippers, whether on a concert stage, in a church sanctuary, or at the grocery store, our effectiveness in this area flows out from that place of connection with God, from the heart.

Another discipline that I engage myself in, especially when I am in a tough spot, is making a new song to the Lord. It keeps me focused on the promise of His commitment to me when it's noisy or my vision of His love gets blurry.

A *souledy* is a term I use to describe my understanding and demonstration of one facet of what the Bible refers to as a "new song." It is a melody that flows from my soul. It is a conscious act of my will that I employ through song to meditate on God. My definition is:

> Souledy: a melodious ode born out of a sacrificial, thankful, meditative, worshipful, reflective, or contemplative heart, resulting in an utterance of a soul (immortal component of a human), that is focused or centered on the character, attributes, or traits of one or more persons of the triune God of Christianity.

In more practical terms, a souledy is a conscious declaration made to the Lord in song. Sometimes, it pours from my heart during fervent communion with God, fierce spiritual warfare, or a moving reflection while simply washing the dishes or folding laundry.

For example, as I would wash those dishes and feel exploited, I just started singing in my heart, "This is not unique to me." The enemy was trying to put space between God and I by influencing my thinking that I was being put upon and not cared for by God. The souledy reminded me of the truth that God had allowed whatever was causing my portion to be what it was; I was not some "special" target. That souledy reminded me that I am a child of the Most High God and the enemy hates us all and will stop at nothing, including self-centered whispering, in effort to put relational space between us and God.

> "Beloved, think it not strange concerning the fiery trial which is to try you, as though some strange thing happened unto you..." (I Peter 4:12, KJV).

I was reaching out to God in faith and although I didn't *feel* like He was watching, singing that little souledy squashed the temptation to believe wrongly. I knew in my spirit that God was near.

I can remember another season of asking God why. I had been trying during this time to get into His presence and nothing—not prayers, a new song, scripture—seemed to get me there. I was tempted to think that I was not connected to God. I was so desperate for a touch from Him and I was working to get Him to commune with me. In truth, I had fallen into a system and began to expect that if a certain time of day, scripture, or song would get me into His presence it always would—like a formula. I was so discouraged when my system failed. I had gotten away from just coming to Him as I was: empty and needing to be filled. Of course with that admission, the "formula" that I was subtly relying on broke and ushered in the presence of the Lord. I was just crying and moaning again, and this time His response came to me in a souledy:

Can You Tell (Why's Answer)

"Can you tell, what I see
I know what you expect from me
It's okay, though you doubt and fear
I love you
I love you
my love!"

When I feel rattled or lost, this souledy still comes to my heart and I feel comforted. God never forsakes His own, regardless of what we may *feel* like. A warm and fuzzy feeling is not proof of God's love. It's the truth—knowing. I appreciate Andrae Crouch's song, "You Don't Have to Jump No Pews (I've Been Born Again)" all the more:

> "You don't have to jump no pews, run down no aisles
> No chills run down your spine
> But you'll know, that you been, born again"

Clinging

There was another spiritual discipline that I grew in my understanding and practice of: fasting. It was a significant contributor toward helping me to see that I was relying on a formula. With the routines of life my prayer life had become the same. The slip into redundancy was snatched out of auto-pilot through the practice fasting.

In his book on the subject, Jentezen Franklin says the following:

> When you fast, your spirit becomes uncluttered by the things of this world and amazingly sensitive to the things of God. Once you've experienced even a glimpse of this and the countless rewards and blessings that follow, it changes your entire perspective.

There are several "types" and "lengths" but in all, Jesus fasted (Luke 4:2-4) and provided us with guidance on fasting (Matthew 6:16; 17:21). If you've never fasted before, just start with turning down something like your morning donut. In that moment when you'd otherwise be enjoying your donut, spend that time in prayer instead. It is a key to reenergize and help focus your faith. Take some time to study more on the discipline of fasting and ask God how much and for how long as well as in such cases, consult proper medical advice.

> "Those who cling to worthless idols turn away from God's love for them" (Jonah 2:8, NIV).

To cling means *to refuse to give something up; to hold onto someone or something tightly.* Clinging is not a passive activity; it is aggressive! Think of a child who wants to be picked up and is clinging to her mama's knee with unyielding tears.

When my children would get exhausted and demand that I pick them up, I could have probably walked around the whole house with them attached to my leg. Through each bumpy step, they would keep clinging until I picked them up and carried them. When you think God isn't *listening* to your prayers, hold on! When you feel *uncomfortable* praying to God, hold on! When you feel awkward without anything of value to say, hold on! This is where the good use of a strong will comes in handy; hold on!

But the key to remember is that it is not your ability to hold on that keeps you near Him; that is just the posture that you must maintain in your heart so that you can see Him. The truth of the matter is that He's got *you* and He will never let you go!

> And I give them eternal life, and they shall never lose it *or* perish throughout the

ages. [To all eternity they shall never by any means be destroyed.] And no one is able to snatch them out of My hand. My Father, Who has given them to Me, is greater *and* mightier than all [else]; and no one is able to snatch [them] out of the Father's hand. I and the Father are One.
John 10:28-30 (AMPC)

I pray that you hop on for that piggyback ride that He is offering to carry you away from all of the things that put distance between you and He. It will be the journey of a lifetime. He wants to love you! That my friend, is the heart of the matter: abandoning our self to trust in the only One who is worthy of and will fulfill our hope.

Hold To God's Unchanging Hand:

"Trust in Him who will not leave you
Whatsoever years may bring
If by earthly friends forsaken
Still more closely to Him cling

Hold to His hand
God's unchanging hand
Build your hopes on things eternal
Hold to God's unchanging hand."

By Mary Jane "Jennie" Bain Wilson (1913)

Therefore we do not lose heart. Though outwardly we are wasting away, yet inwardly we are being renewed day by day. For our light and momentary troubles are achieving for us an eternal glory that far outweighs them all. So we fix our eyes not on what is seen, but on what is unseen, since what is seen is temporary, but what is unseen is eternal.

        2 Corinthians 4:16-18 (NIV)

Chapter Eight

Watch Out!

"Then said the LORD, Doest thou well to be angry?"
                                    Jonah 4:4 (KJV)

The enemy is a jealous space hog and is not going to be very happy that you are in a close relationship with the Lord. He is actually going to passionately hate it because there is no space for him!

There is no need to fear *this* but do watch out and be aware.

The Jonah Syndrome

Jonah went to Nineveh as God requested him to do. He declared God's Words as God directed him to and the Ninevites repented. So what got Jonah so bent out of shape? Here is a paraphrase of the passage that explains the reason:

> Jonah was furious. He lost his temper. He yelled at GOD, "GOD! I knew it—when I

> was back home, I knew this was going to happen! That's why I ran off to Tarshish! I knew you were sheer grace and mercy, not easily angered, rich in love, and ready at the drop of a hat to turn your plans of punishment into a program of forgiveness! 'So, GOD, if you won't kill them, kill me! I'm better off dead!'
>
> Jonah 4:1-3 (MSG)

Wow! Wasn't his mission a success? How could Jonah be angry over the positive results of his evangelistic crusade? Easy, he looked around at people in judgment and comparison instead of looking up at God, the incomparable righteous judge. Jonah lost proper focus. Comparison is carnality and plumps your flesh appetizingly as prey for the space hog. He will use our natural inclination of self-centeredness as a means to create space between you and God. Jonah was so busy looking at others but where he needed to look was in the mirror.

> "Or do you think lightly of the riches of His kindness and tolerance and patience, not knowing that the kindness of God leads you to repentance?" (Romans 2:4, NASB).

How quickly Jonah forgot about the kindness and tolerance and patience that God extended to him!

God protected him from a certain death by drowning. God provided a miraculous fish that protected him from the harmful elements of the raging waters. God provided another opportunity for Jonah to respond to God's call to go and preach to the Ninevites. God did not throw Jonah away and remained committed to him.

All that Jonah was supposed to do was deliver God's message and yet this one task that God requested that he perform turned into this incredible drama!

Funny that Jonah's name means dove. Immediately my thoughts are drawn to the account in the book of Genesis, where a dove was used as a messenger of sorts to inform Noah of the flooding status, after it rained upon the earth for forty days and nights.

> Then he sent out a dove from him, to see if the water was abated from the face of the land; but the dove found no resting place for the sole of her foot, so she returned to him into the ark, for the water was on the surface of all the earth. Then he put out his hand and took her, and brought her into the ark to himself. So he waited yet another seven days; and again he sent out the dove from the ark. The dove came to him toward evening, and behold, in her beak was a freshly picked olive leaf. So Noah knew that the water was abated from the earth. Then he waited yet another seven days, and sent out the dove; but she did not return to him again.
>
> Genesis 8:8-12 (NASB)

Jesus wasn't self-centered. His life on earth was not just about maintaining His close relationship with the Father, He was about taking care of the Father's business: loving people.

Jonah was invited to engage in the Father's business and we, His children, are invited to engage in the family business too: loving people. As children of God, we reflect Him, represent Him, and are to be His messengers of love.

> "And he said unto them, How is it that ye sought me? wist ye not that I must be about my Father's business?" (Luke 2:49, KJV).

> "For even the Son of Man did not come to be served, but to serve, and to give his life as a ransom for many" (Mark 10:45, NIV).

> "Again Jesus said, "Peace be with you! As the Father has sent me, I am sending you." (John 20:21, NIV).

It is tempting to resent any acts of kindness and mercy that God shows towards those that hurt us or that for whatever reason we don't believe deserve His merciful and gracious treatment. God is not like us. He doesn't struggle with what we struggle with though He understands. The difference is that He sees, knows, and understands everything, not just in light of today but in light of eternity.

PROGRESS KEY: Be a conduit of God's mercy, especially to those who do not know Him personally and beware of self-centeredness and self-righteousness, which are traps used by the space hog!

> The Lord is not slack concerning his promise, as some men count slackness;

> but is longsuffering to us-ward, not willing that any should perish, but that all should come to repentance.
>
> 2 Peter 3:9 (KJV)

God Usues Kindness

When selfish anger at God's grace and mercy given to another is present in a child and servant of God, I call it a bad case of the *Jonah Syndrome*. When you fall prey to this condition, you lose focus, insight, and vision.

Are there some folks that should not receive God's grace and mercy from the Lord? Do we forget God's mercy toward us too quickly and selfishly resent when He doles out gobs of it to people of whom we don't think deserve it?

Honestly, I don't know anyone who is ecstatic when they see God's hand blessing people that they don't believe deserve it. As this was a challenge for me, I want to share with you a few ways that I was able to navigate through the *Jonah Syndrome* and not fall prey to the trap of the *space hog!*

It can be hard for us to accept that God's judgments are always a reflection of a person's heart. It's hard because we can't see a person's heart though we can clearly see their behavior. Our inclination to judge the state of someone's heart based upon their behavior often leads us to the wrong conclusion and disappointment with God.

PROGRESS KEY: Look trustingly at our incomparable God and don't fall prey to the temptation of assessing another's value and comparing their worthiness against your finite measuring stick. When we do this, the *space hog* exploits this opportunity to create relational distance between us and God.

The Jonah Syndrome shows us something about our flesh. We like things that bless and benefit us, especially if we didn't have to do anything to bring it about. Isn't that what grace is—our divine benefits earned by God at Christ's expense?

The problem comes in when our natural desire to exercise our prideful will rises up. In this situation, we want to be consulted and ultimately in charge of selecting who, what, when, and how much of God's grace and mercy that He extends to others. This is magnified all the more when He has called us to be the one to deliver these divine benefits to those we consider undeserving.

This tendency causes a troublesome hesitation as we extend our period of finite reasoning. This period of reasoning only makes us judgmental, not wise, sovereign, or gracious. As Dietrich Bonhoeffer puts it in his book, *The Cost of Discipleship:*

> Judging others makes us blind, whereas love is illuminating. By judging others we blind ourselves to our own evil and to the grace which others are just as entitled to as we are.

Guard against the *space hog!*

Take The High Road!

I've grown to appreciate the high road; it's less congested than the low one. The high road is one way that I navigated through the Jonah Syndrome.

Jesus, as our model, showed us this as He strove to align His flesh with the Father's will in the Garden of Gethsemane.

If Jesus did not bow His knee in reverent submission to God's call and go to the cross, we would all be lost. We would be without hope. Jesus was intentional and purposeful about going to the cross. He loved His father and taking care of His Father's business, which was and still is loving people.

> "Saying, Father, if thou be willing, remove this cup from me: nevertheless not my will, but thine, be done" (Luke 22:42, KJV).

It is often difficult to submit our will to the will of God when the pathway ahead is certain to be unpleasant! Why? Because often obeying His will surely cost us more than our self-centered nature is willing to pay. Our self-centeredness is strong and desires to drive our lives with its own selfish desires!

> So I say, live by the Spirit, and you will not gratify the desires of the sinful nature. For the sinful nature desires what is contrary to the Spirit, and the Spirit what is contrary to the sinful nature. They are in conflict with each other, so that you do not do what you want.
> Galatians 5:16-17 (NIV)

You have advantage over the enemy. You are not without the power tools to guard against his traps and snares aimed at putting relational space between you and God. Note that he never stops at aggressively attempting to wiggle some space in there. He is a relentless space hog *always* looking for opportunity!

> "Submit yourselves therefore to God. Resist the devil, and he will flee from you" (James 4:7, KJV).

PROGRESS KEY: Respond to God's call in humble submission, promptly and exactly; that is your power tool!

> Be well balanced (temperate, sober of mind), be vigilant *and* cautious at all times; for that enemy of yours, the devil, roams around like a lion roaring [[a]in fierce hunger], seeking someone to seize upon *and* devour. Withstand him; be firm in faith [against his onset—rooted, established, strong, immovable, and determined], knowing that the same ([b] identical) sufferings are appointed to your brotherhood (the whole body of Christians) throughout the world.
> 1 Peter 5:8-9 (AMPC)

It is not a mysterious thing as to how to resist the devil which will cause him to flee away from you. The Spirit of God does not sweep over you and suddenly the devil disappears—no! You resist the devil by the conscious acts of your will and obedient behavior to God. If you are double-minded, fickle and indecisive, he will also exploit that space in your decision making.

> For the time being no discipline brings joy, but seems grievous *and* painful; but afterwards it yields a peaceable fruit of righteousness to those who have been trained by it [a harvest of fruit which consists in righteousness—in conformity to God's will in purpose, thought, and action, resulting in right living and right standing with God].
>
> Hebrews 12:11 (AMPC)

PROGRESS KEY: Do right on purpose! Other people are not the problem, as evidenced by the following verse.

> For we wrestle not against flesh and blood, but against principalities, against powers, against the rulers of the darkness of this world, against spiritual wickedness in high places.
>
> Ephesians 6:12 (KJV)

We're all vulnerable to losing sight of the real enemy, trying to use and do whatever he can to wedge space in our relationship with God, but let's remain mindful that we are not defenseless; be intentional!

> But the fruit of the Spirit is love, joy, peace, forbearance, kindness, goodness, faithfulness, gentleness and self-control. Against such things there is no law. Those who belong to Christ Jesus have crucified the flesh with its passions and desires. Since we live by the Spirit, let us

> keep in step with the Spirit. Let us not become conceited, provoking and envying each other.
> Galatians 5:22-26 (NIV)

Again, the urge to do right does not happen by the Spirit of God mysteriously sweeping over you and voila! It happens by intentional decision making and conscious acts of your will.

Like with fruit, in an overly simplistic illustration, it is the result of allowing the free-flow of sap to rise from the nutrient-rich roots, enabling it to nourish the branches from which the fruit is sustained and securely grows from.

Similarly, when we allow the spirit of God to rule our lives through our intentional, reverent submission to His words, His will, and His ways, it nourishes us from the inside and we bear this good spiritual fruit on the outside as a result of being an uncluttered, yielded conduit.

Not Fair!

If any groom has the right to divorce His bride, it is Christ. He has had to put up with His bride, the church (you and me)! He is the consummate model of unconditional love. You may be saying "He's God, though." But because He is God and He is all-knowing, He knows what we can handle, and in His wisdom, He would not call us in a way that we were incapable to respond to apart from Him. But we can only respond with His help, with His perspective, and with His Love.

We have committed adultery time and time again! We have lied, talked Him down, stolen money from Him, held more than one love in our heart, gave what He provided to our other lover, killed His children, and yet He loves us still! All as if we did none of those things at all.

He still looks at us longingly with great affection, passion and love. The twinkle is still in His eyes for us. He holds nothing back from us. He speaks and protects us and courts us still. He brags on us and shows us off because He is proud of us yet all the while He knows us through and through!

In light of this, why is it so hard for us to forgive one another?

In his book *The Gift of Forgiveness*, Dr. Charles Stanley explains that the cycle of forgiveness begins when an offense is committed, a debt is owed, and then forgiveness is the cancellation of that debt.

Unforgiveness is cruel. It forces the offended to carry around something that is dead, gone, and in the past. This is similar to one type of torturous punishment to which murderers in ancient times were sentenced.

A person convicted of murder had to bear the body of his victim affixed in some fashion to his own body and had to carry that body around with him. As the body of the victim decayed and became infested with maggots, mites, etc., it infected the murderer as well and caused him to die an agonizing, slow, horrible death.

> Centuries ago, some Roman emperors were known to inflict the hideous punishment of binding the corpse of a murder victim to the back of the murderer. Under penalty of death, no one was allowed to remove the body from the condemned person.
> *Our Daily Bread* (March 27, 1999)

The spirit of unforgiveness is a lot like that. As you lug around offenses, they become toxic and infest you. You can only pretend for so long that you are not being affected by the dead thing you are lugging around before you begin to reek of toxicity so much that people run the other way when they see you coming. "Stinky!" they scream. Their response can create even more bitterness in one walking in unforgiveness.

PROGRESS KEY: It is true that though you can forgive an offense, the mere hope (not guarantee) of restoration of the relationship with the offender can only be realized when they have repented and confessed the truth.

Transformed

I don't see God the same as I did before—and no, it is not because I got any of that rejection residue in my eyes from being spit up ashore.

After all that we have been through, what is there to fret over? He forgives me and loves me. I will not carry a burden of guilt or unforgiveness because I don't have to and neither do you. I am whole and acceptable to God because of the act of reverent submission by Christ to live a perfect life and be crucified on the cross.

> What shall we then say to these things? If God be for us, who can be against us? He that spared not his own Son, but delivered him up for us all, how shall he not with him also freely give us all things? Who shall lay any thing to the charge of God's elect? It is God that jus-

tifieth. Who is he that condemneth? It is Christ that died, yea rather, that is risen again, who is even at the right hand of God, who also maketh intercession for us. Who shall separate us from the love of Christ? shall tribulation, or distress, or persecution, or famine, or nakedness, or peril, or sword? As it is written, For thy sake we are killed all the day long; we are accounted as sheep for the slaughter. Nay, in all these things we are more than conquerors through him that loved us. For I am persuaded, that neither death, nor life, nor angels, nor principalities, nor powers, nor things present, nor things to come, Nor height, nor depth, nor any other creature, shall be able to separate us from the love of God, which is in Christ Jesus our Lord.

Romans 8:31-39 (KJV)

Now what?

You must forgive me for craving the proverbial *happy ending* to this drama-filled book of the Bible, but honestly I found the ending of the book to be anti-climactic!

Only silence from Jonah?

I was waiting for a big altar call with Jonah bolting down the sanctuary aisle with tears streaming down his face and his hair flying in the breeze, testifying about how he wound up in the fish's belly through the grace of God's protection and how he was spit up and given another chance to get it right. I wanted to see Jonah, enlisting in frontline duty in the Lord's Army but…no such thing happened!

That's how it all ends: silence!

So I ask you, my friend, how will you respond to the Lord? *Your* Lord!

What are you going to do in response to His call to you, in response to His forgiveness, mercy and unmerited grace towards you?

Will you let God love you?

Right there in your heart, even as you are holding these pages, I pray that you say yes to the Lord. Oh the journey to love that awaits you. Climb up into God's lap and hear His heartbeat for you.

So go ahead and put an exclamation point on the freedom you have found. Your testimony is so powerful, no matter how bizarre it may appear on the outside because someone if not many are waiting for you to tell it and need to hear it.

I would encourage you to share your testimony of journeying with the Lord with someone. It will provide a reminder and encouragement to you as you recall how God indeed brought you out of the belly of your great fish, whatever detailed form that may have been and drew you closer to Himself.

Additionally, during those moments when the enemy tempts you with the thought that perhaps your relationship with Christ isn't really close or that God is not really committed to you, your testimony refreshes your declarations of the mighty works of God in your life and the custom way He personally delivered you unto Himself!

Testify of your firsthand knowledge of His initiation and passionate desire to provide you with the security and freedom that only a walk with Him can bring. Share the stories of His patient and comforting care and how He has been with you and never abandoned you during a single step you've taking during your journey, even when it didn't *feel* as though He was near.

Go ahead and boldly celebrate the promises of God in your life with the fruit of your lips!

I will testify that I am God's beloved daughter:

- God is Love
- He loves you
- He loves me

> "And they overcame him by the blood of the Lamb, and by the word of their testimony; and they loved not their lives unto the death" (Revelations 12:11, KJV).

"Journey Journal"

*Print Your Name:*_____.

"Keep thy heart with all diligence; for out of it are the issues of life" (Proverbs 4:23, KJV).

It is so important in our busy world that we take the time to *keep* our heart. Through prayer and a yielded heart before God, journaling is one way to help accomplish this.

My prayer is that your Journey Journal becomes more than a series of informational replies but rather invested sentiments from your heart. As you review each chapter, my hope is that it challenges and provokes you to draw closer to God, as you journey through this life and that it foster the habits of:

- Listening to your heart
- Quickly and critically assessing its condition
- Providing the necessary boundaries and resources for the spiritual growth and health of your heart

Are you walking with God? If not, join with Him today! Travel to the back of

JANEEN MICHAEL

this journal and learn how. All aboard…
weigh anchor…let's start sailing!
"Journey Journal"

Based on the book, *Journey to Love,* by Janeen Michael

Chapter Review Guide

Described below are the seven sections for each Chapter Review:

1. Chapter Focus: Listed here will be a quote to provide a general discussion and review of the corresponding chapter in the book *Journey to Love*. You will be asked to comment with your thoughts on the selected quote.

2. Mirror Check: This is an ice breaker exercise that will make the book content more familiar and personal to you. In a group setting, responses can be verbal but should be independently journaled, too.

3. Weigh Anchor: This section will provoke greater personal discovery as you will be asked to select two statements to respond to in depth.

4. Throw Overboard: Activities will be provided in this section to further engage you and promote your personal application of things you've discovered and learned in the previous sections.

5. From the Belly: An opportunity is given in this section to saturate your journey with focused prayer.

There will be topics of prayer assigned, requiring a thoughtful written response in your Journey Journal.

6. Journey Journal: Finally, go for it! This is your section to talk about *your journey* with the Lord.

7. Chart Your Course: This section will give recommended preparations for the next Chapter Review.

Tip: To achieve maximum effectiveness, be honest before God and be honest to yourself, as you record in your Journey Journal.

Chapter One Review

Selective Hearing

1. Chapter Focus: *"...I was experiencing distance in my relationship with God; like He was giving me the cold shoulder or the silent treatment and it hurt bad."* After reading this quote from Chapter One of the book *Journey To Love*, what thoughts surface to your mind as you reflect on your journey with the Lord?

2. Mirror Check: Review the definition of *ish-you* from Chapter One. Tell of one *ish-you* that you are currently facing.

3. Weigh Anchor: Respond to two from the following:
   a) Whether or not you journal regularly, explain the benefit it will provide.
   b) Many have expressed a fear of journaling stating, "What if *someone* finds it?" Is this a Godly fear and faith-filled response? Explain.
   c) What aspect or dimension of intimacy do you desire to have with God that you haven't achieved yet? What do you believe the hindrance to be?
   d) Do you feel worthy of God's unconditional love? Why or why not?
   e) Give an example of how you see God loving you unconditionally today.
   f) Name a time when you subjected yourself to mistreatment because you believed or were coerced to believe that it would bring you a positive result. What was the positive result you were hoping for?
   g) What practical decisions, with your lifestyle and schedule, are you empowered to make that will unencumber your schedule and allow you to spend consecrated time with God every day?
   h) Do you have "turmoil" in your life that is disrupting your peace? What choices are you empowered to make, right now, that will establish needed boundaries to effectively remedy this?
   i) Have you ever needed supernatural help but felt like you would be inconveniencing God and *burdening* Him with your plea?

j) Has the enemy ever successfully made you feel guilty for needing God's help along your journey? How did this impact your ability to draw intimately near God?

4. Throw Overboard: Draw a picture or describe in detail, the features of a mask you wear most often. Explain what this mask was intended to provide or offer you coverage for/from.

5. From the Belly: To remove a mask, you must tell the truth about what the mask is. Write down a record of confession to God regarding your masking behavior. Ask God to reveal strongholds in your heart that cause you to be hampered in drawing closer to Him.

6. Journey Journal: My journey with the Lord... (Continue this thought)

7. Chart your Course: Meditate on Psalm 139:14 and read chapter two in, *Journey to Love*.

"I will praise thee; for I am fearfully and wonderfully made: marvelous are thy works; and that my soul knoweth right well" (Psalm 139:14, KJV).

Chapter Two Review

Tag! You're It!

1. Chapter Focus: "*Why run and hide from God's call? It really is a finite-thinking response to do such a thing.*" After reading this quote from Chapter Two, what thoughts surface to your mind as you reflect on your journey with the Lord?

2. Mirror Check: Describe a time when you felt like God didn't love you.

3. Weigh Anchor: Respond to two from the following:
   a) Does your perception of who the All-Knowing, All-Powerful God is, tempt you to put on a "mask" or to disrobe in His presence?
   b) How can a comfort zone be harmful as it relates to growing in an intimate, dynamic relationship with Christ? Are there any harmful comfort zones in your life now?
   c) From the eagle lesson, recall a time when God was seemingly standing by and watching you "test your wings." Did you feel alone or embraced? Explain.
   d) How would you define "masking behavior"? Masks are ultimately nothing more than false barriers. How is/are your mask(s) shielding you or blocking you from receiving what you need from God? Explain.
   e) Masks can originate from different sources. What is the primary source of your masks

and why do you believe they were provided or offered to you?

f) Read Psalm 5:12. God's favor is not because of who you are but whose you are. God's favor is not because of what you do but because of what God has done in that He has made us righteous. How does this verse foster a greater trust in God?

g) Are there any violations in your life that you have been in denial about? Do you trust that God will repay the perpetrators for what they've done? How does your trust in God enable you to let go of wrongful things people have done to you?

h) To isolate violating experiences and keep them from running rampant in your life, what spiritual disciplines e.g., prayer, reading the Bible, meditating on scriptures, etc., will help you the most and why?

i) Describe a time when your perception of God's grace and mercy being extended toward one that seemed undeserving of it, created a crisis of belief for you in God's character as a righteous judge?

j) Is there one challenging area or relationship in your life that you are currently responding to in a way that demonstrates/suggests a lack of trust in God's love for you? Explain.

4. Throw overboard: We are all prone to run and hide from God's call when it doesn't align with our expectations. The following is what I call the "Spiral Exercise" which helps us outline the wind-

ing pattern our lives take when we are responding waywardly to God's call. Using a scenario from your own life, outline a spiraled course that your life took on, as I've done below, as a result of responding waywardly to God's call:

God asked me to: Smile at my mean next-door neighbor.
The internal conflict & struggle: Feelings of shame because I've gossiped about this neighbor to my other neighbor who lives on the other side of me.
The external conflict & struggle: My gossip buddy may call me a hypocrite for smiling at the mean neighbor.
Decision making skewed from center: I'll obey God if my neighbor smiles at me first.
Behavior skewed from center: Peeking out of window to make sure that I avoid neighbor when I leave my house.

Now you record your own personal example.
God asked me to:_____
The internal conflict and struggle:_____
The external conflict and struggle:_____
Decision making skewed from center:__
Behavior skewed from center:_____

5. From the Belly: Write a prayer to God asking Him to show you more of Himself, for the courage to trust His righteousness and precepts, and to keep you following along in the path of His solid footsteps.

6. Journey Journal: My journey with the Lord... (Continue this thought)

7. Chart Your Course: Meditate on Hebrews 4:13 and read chapter three in *Journey to Love*.

   "Nothing in all creation is hidden from God's sight. Everything is uncovered and laid bare before the eyes of him to whom we must give account" (Hebrews 4:13, NIV).

Chapter Three Review

Jump Already!

1. Chapter Focus: *"The longer we delay in responding to God with a yes and hop aboard, our finite reasoning and logic tends to get the best of us and takes over the helm, directing our path."* After reading this quote from Chapter Three, what thoughts surface to your mind as you reflect on your journey with the Lord?

2. Mirror Check: Name a modified/contrived behavior you performed, like becoming a "do-bot" or some other action to secure the affirmation of a person or persons, though the affirmation you sought could only be secured by God.

3. Weigh Anchor: Respond to two from the following:
   a) Examine the most recent time that you perceived God's lack of response toward you to be

like that of a preoccupied parent. How did you respond to God? Did you throw a tantrum, patiently wait, or something else? Explain.

b) Isaiah 55:9 says, "For as the heavens are higher than the earth, so are my ways higher than your ways and my thoughts than your thoughts (KJV)." Describe an occasion when you figured out and executed a way out of a challenging situation that circumvented the known precepts of God. What was the result?

c) In this *microwave age,* are you often tempted to interact with God as if you are in a short-term relationship or long-term relationship? Explain.

d) What would you consider to be your dominant temperament type, e.g., loyal, leader, outgoing, kind-hearted, etc.? When you don't submit this trait under God's control, describe how the negative side of your temperament manifests itself.

e) The concept of a "do-bot" was introduced in Chapter Three. Have you devised a set of behaviors that compromise or reduce what God made you to be in effort to secure the attention of an individual or group of persons? What aspect of God's plan for your life is being compromised or reduced?

f) Is it difficult to be honest and truthful, at the expense of unity, when facing a challenge in your most significant relationships? Why or why not?

g) Is your heart pliable enough toward God so that you can receive correction from Him as it relates to wrong behaviors, and mindsets that you are adhering to that go against the instruction of scripture? Describe. Write down any family, cultural, social, religious, or other traditions that you participate in that facilitate or foster behaviors and mindsets that are in contradiction with scripture.

h) Read Psalm 127:1-2. Many people place their faith and trust in earthly resources to meet their needs. According to these verses, how can earthly resources create a false sense of security?

i) Read 1 Peter 5:7. Are there any cares in your life, hampering your relational closeness with the Lord? If so, what are they? How will *letting go* of these cares draw you closer to the Lord and rid you of anxiety?

j) "Please God and He'll take care of the consequences." Do you believe this statement is true? If so, do you live your life as if this statement is true? Why or why not?

4. Throw Overboard Make one chart with two columns. In the column on the left, list five things that cause you to fear or doubt God's unconditional love for you. In the column on the right, refute that fear or doubt you listed on the left with an attribute of God's character or with a passage of scripture.

5. From the Belly: Write a short prayer to God asking Him to remove fear and doubt, increase your faith in Him, and for the strength and wisdom needed to submit your temperament under His authority.

6. Journey Journal: My journey with the Lord... (Continue this thought)

7. Chart your course: Meditate on John 8:32 and read chapter four in *Journey to Love*.

"Then you will know the truth, and the truth will set you free" (John 8:32, NIV).

Chapter Four Review

In Over My Head!

1. Chapter Focus: *"The piggyback ride away from my fears and unbelief started out very bumpy. He was holding me but I also needed to get used to holding on to Him too; it helped make the ride smoother."* After reading this quote from Chapter Four, what thoughts surface to your mind as you reflect on your journey with the Lord?

2. Mirror Check: What is your unfiltered response to pain that you have or are possibly currently experiencing that you have no control to stop?

3. Weigh Anchor: Respond to two from the following:
   a) Do you draw closer to God or away from Him when realistic expectations of those most significant to you go unmet and you receive rejection from them instead? What disciplines could you implement to consistently draw

you closer to God during those disappointing moments?

b) One definition for the word affinity is "an attraction to or liking for something." What do you believe is God's affinity toward you? Is there a scripture you can provide to support your response?

c) Have you ever engaged in self-destructive behavior in effort to take control of a situation or circumstance? Explain.

d) All people have legitimate physical needs. Describe a time when you resorted to an illegitimate (ungodly) method to provide for this need. What was the result?

e) All people have legitimate emotional needs. Describe a time when you resorted to an illegitimate (ungodly) way to provide for this need. What was the result?

f) Can you recall a specific time in your life when God was silent or appeared indifferent to your need? Did you wait for God to provide for you in His way or not? What was the result?

g) How is God's way different from the "world's way" of getting our need for feeling valued met? Have you ever sought to get this need met apart from God's way? How did you go about it? What was the result of your pursuit?

h) Answer one of the five questions that the sailors asked Jonah. Explain how your response exposes where you may be prone to fear, unbelief, or a particular ish-you in your relationship with God.

i) Describe how God's affirmation of you connects your spiritual reality to your earthly experience and further keeps you from feeling fragmented and lost.
   j) How do you emotionally balance yourself to allow your focus for approval to be based on what God thinks of you versus what people may think of you?

4. Throw Overboard: To enable success, we need a plan. Write down your plan for avoiding involvement with the following: Quarreling, jealousy, anger, hostility, slander, gossip, conceit, disorder, and sexual immorality.

5. Prayer Focus: Write a prayer asking God to draw you closer to Him and remove things that you see that are attempting to pull you away from Him; creating relational distance and space. Ask God for the strength needed to abandon all elements of self that keep you from trusting Him implicitly to meet your needs. Finally, ask God for patience to wait for His response to your prayer.

6. Journey Journal: My journey with the Lord… (Continue this thought)

7. Chart Your Course: Mediate on Psalm 147:3 and read chapter four in *Journey to Love*.

"He heals the brokenhearted and binds up their wounds" (Psalm 147:3, NIV).

Chapter Five Review

Let Me Help You!

1. Chapter Focus: *"Yes, affliction is like a nutcracker; it applies pressure in our lives to reveal what's on the inside of us."* After reading this quote from Chapter Five, what thoughts surface to your mind as you reflect on your journey with the Lord?

2. Mirror Check: Among other reasons, God provided a whale for Jonah to create an environment where He had Jonah's undivided attention. In effort to reveal what work you can and should do to close relational distance between you and God, what situation or circumstance did God allow to capture your undivided attention?

3. Weigh Anchor: Respond to two from the following:
   a) Recall a time when God used affliction to reveal a hardened, brittle or rotten area of your heart? What form of affliction did He use? When the affliction presented itself, was it a surprise? Explain.
   b) As you look back on a case of affliction that God allowed to come your way, could you see the rotten, brittle, or hardened area of your heart before the affliction revealed it to a greater degree? Explain.
   c) Though it may not have been fleeing to Tarshish, describe a time that you attempted to run and hide from God's call to you. What was the result?

d) When you survey the things that you naturally like and gravitate towards, which of those things are most difficult to turn away from if required to hear God's still small voice? Explain.
e) What are the most common external struggles that are revealed when choosing to respond to God's call? How can you increase your sensitivity to God's still small voice in the midst of those frequent external struggles?
f) What are the most common internal struggles that are revealed when choosing to respond to God's call? How can you increase your sensitivity to God's still small voice in the midst of those frequent internal struggles?
g) Detail something that God asked you to do and you disobeyed. Did you eventually repent, obey, and embrace the forgiveness of God? Explain.
h) Has a brittle, hardened, or rotten area of your heart been revealed and you didn't have enough strength to apply the pressure needed to confront it and repent of it? Explain.
i) Recall something you learned about God during a time of affliction? Explain.
j) Choose one person in your life that has taught you both what to do and not to do. Explain what it is that they modeled that taught you each of these lessons.

4. Throw Overboard: For one full day (preferably a weekday) make a record of how you spend your time. At the end of that day, examine how much

down time you had and how you spent it. Did you make the same effort to seek God regularly in a concerted way, as you did with other people and commitments?

5. Prayer Focus: Write a prayer to God asking Him to help you maintain transparency with the Him, compassion towards others, and to always be mindful of the price Christ paid for your liberty.

6. Journey Journal: My journey with the Lord... (Continue this thought)

7. Chart Your Course: Mediate on Psalm 51:10-12 and read chapter six in *Journey to Love*.

Create in me a pure heart, O God, and renew a steadfast spirit within me. Do not cast me from your presence or take your Holy Spirit from me. Restore to me the joy of your salvation and grant me a willing spirit, to sustain me.
Psalm 51:10-12 (NIV)

Chapter Six Review

Spit Up Ashore

1. Chapter Focus: *"Now that the hemorrhaging stopped and the healing was progressing, I needed to begin walking, demonstrating my faith in God; like physical therapy that helps recover and return your strength."*

After reading this quote from Chapter Six, what thoughts surface to your mind as you reflect on your journey with the Lord?

2. Mirror Check: Have you ever spent consecrated time with the Lord and it caused a change in you that was unmistakably noticeable to others? Share this experience.

3. Weigh Anchor: Respond to two from the following:
   a) Have you ever faced a time of being alone to the point that friends, family, or coworkers and others avoided you *like a plague*? Did this time of isolation find you drawing closer to God or drifting away from Him? Explain.
   b) Have you ever had strongholds in your pattern of behavior or thinking that required an extra measure of God's power for you to remove them? Explain.
   c) Do you find it a challenge to trust that God alone will provide for all of your needs? Are certain needs more difficult to trust that He will meet than with others? Explain.
   d) How do you open your hand to God and release to Him all of those things that could cause you to be overcome with fear and unbelief?
   e) "Fake it 'til you make it." How can this approach be unwise?
   f) "Practice makes perfect" vs. "practice makes habits." From your own personal experience, explain why the second statement is more accurate than the first.

g) Explain what aspect of Christ's character do you find the easiest to imitate. Explain what aspects of Christ's character you find the most challenging to imitate.
h) What does it mean for you to trust in the unconditional love of God? Is this always easy for you to do? Why or why not?
i) How can harboring feelings of guilt hamper you from progressing along in your journey with the Lord?
j) Describe a time when you courageously demonstrated your faith in God. How did it transform you?

4. Throw Overboard: List your most critical area in the blank. Please enter more than one, if needed. Loving myself as God does means releasing _____ and handing it over to God.

5. Prayer Focus: Write a prayer to God thanking Him for the indwelling power of His spirit living on the inside of you that enables you to demonstrate your faith in Him which is transforming you into the image of Christ.

6. Journey Journal: My journey with the Lord… (Continue this thought)

7. Chart Your Course: Meditate on Galatians 5:1 and read chapter seven in *Journey to Love*.

"It is for freedom that Christ has set us free. Stand firm, then, and do not let yourselves

be burdened again by a yoke of slavery" (Galatians 5:1, NIV).

Chapter Seven Review

Heart & Song of the Matter

1. Chapter Focus: *"Prayer is simply having a conversation with God by both talking and listening... The more I prayed the more at peace I felt."* After reading this quote from Chapter Seven, what thoughts surface to your mind as you reflect on your journey with the Lord?

2. Mirror Check: Out of the following four, which spiritual discipline is the easiest for you to maintain: Worship, Bible study, prayer, fasting. Explain your answer.

3. Weigh Anchor: Respond to two from the following:
   a) How is it that your uprightness before God can sometimes be an offense to others?
   b) Why is prayer so crucial to our relationship with God?
   c) What has consecrated prayer done for your walk with the Lord and your ability to see the pathway ahead more clearly?
   d) How is knowing scripture critical in your ability to communicate with God?
   e) Read Psalm 119:11. Do you have a habit of memorizing scripture? If so, do you find it easy to memorize scripture or difficult? Explain what makes it easy or difficult for you.

f) Read Psalm 40:9-10. Recall the first time or most recent time that you poured your soul out to God in public prayer. What impact did this experience have on your relationship with God?

g) Conversation occurs through speaking and listening. Do you pray expecting that your conversation with God will be clear and understandable? Do you believe God hears you when you pray and do you believe you can hear God when He speaks to you? Explain.

h) Read Psalm 150:1-6. Do you worship God freely in song and dance? Why or why not? What element is needed for you to achieve uninhibited worship?

i) Is it easy or difficult to embrace God's right to control our lives through requiring our obedience to His Word? How is not allowing God the right to control your life a form of self-destruction?

j) Have you ever fallen into a "system" of getting into God's presence by using a specific prayer, song, or Bible verse that failed you? Explain the system in detail and describe the moment it stopped working for you? How did you turn it around and break free of that system to be found in His presence again?

4. Throw Overboard: Choose four scripture verses recited anywhere in this book that have spoken most to your heart. Take an index card for each verse (or small piece of paper) and write the verse on one side and the scripture reference on the other

side. For example, the first side will have the verse such as "Jesus wept" and then flipping the card or piece of paper over on the opposite side you will write the Bible reference, which in this example would be John 11:35. Make a card for each of the four verses. Spend a few moments each day reciting the verse on the card and then without looking at the card, quote the scripture reference, memorizing what it says. Continue reviewing and practicing until you can memorize the verse and scripture reference.

5. Prayer Focus: Write a prayer to God asking Him to show you areas of your heart that you have not made pliable before Him. Write God a poem or letter confessing your love and gratefulness to Him.

6. Journey Journal: My journey with the Lord… (Continue this thought)

7. Chart Your Course: Meditate on Psalm 16:11 and read Chapter Eight in *Journey to Love*.

"Thou wilt shew me the path of life: in thy presence is fullness of joy; at thy right hand there are pleasures for evermore" (Psalm 16:11, KJV).

Chapter Eight Review

Watch Out

1. Chapter Focus: *"Be a conduit of God's mercy, especially to those who do not know Him personally and beware of self-centeredness and self-righteousness, which are traps used by the space hog."* After reading this quote from Chapter Eight, what thoughts surface to your mind as you reflect on your journey with the Lord?

2. Mirror Check: Recall a time when you ignored the voice of God and turned down an opportunity to encourage or help someone because you didn't believe that they deserved it.

3. Weigh Anchor: Respond to two from the following:
   a) "The Jonah Syndrome" was a concept introduced to identify selfish anger at God's mercy toward another. How can having this attitude hamper your progressively deepening relationship with the Lord?
   b) When you see God's mercy doled out upon someone that you don't believe deserves it, does it cause you to lose sight of the miraculous quantities of mercy that He has bestowed upon you? Explain.
   c) God eroded the gourd plant to expose Jonah's selfish heart. Has God eroded something in your life that exposed selfishness in your heart? If so, were you able to see God's hand in the erosion process initially? Explain.

d) Like Jonah who sat and watched what would become of the city, have you ever stopped moving forward, due to your attention being focused on what God was doing in someone else's life? Explain.
e) What types of people make you prone to harbor selfish anger in your heart? How can you reverse this tendency?
f) How would maintaining a thankful heart toward God help insulate you from falling prey to the Jonah Syndrome?
g) What are some of the ways that you have resisted the devil and denied the space hog the opportunity to put relational space between you and God?
h) What are some of the ways that you can guard against the space hog?
i) Read Matthew 5:44. How is forgiving someone a demonstration of your faith and trust in God? Do you pray for your enemies? Why or why not? What benefit does it serve to pray for your enemies?
j) Name several benefits that you and others receive as a result of you sharing your testimony?

4. Throw Overboard:
If your personal journal was lost and found by someone that does not have a relationship with the Lord, write an entry in your journal now that tells them what they're missing from not having an intimate relationship with Christ. Encourage them

in your entry to embark upon a journey with the Lord.

5. Prayer Focus:
    Write a prayer of thanksgiving to God for His proven commitment to loving you and for more opportunities to share the testimony of your journey with the Lord.

6. Journey Journal: My journey with the Lord... (Continue this thought)

7. Chart Your Course: Meditate on Psalm 71:18.

I will go in the strength of the Lord GOD: I will make mention of thy righteousness, even of thine only. O God, thou hast taught me from my youth: and hitherto have I declared thy wondrous works. Now also when I am old and grey-headed, O God, forsake me not; until I have shewed thy strength unto this generation, and thy power to everyone that is to come.
Psalm 71:16-18 (KJV)

Bibliography

Asshur and the land of Nimrod by Hormuzd Rassam. Publication date October 31, 2015. ASIN: B017GDC6CS

Assyrian History: A Captivating Guide to the Assyrians and Their Powerful Empire in Ancient Mesopotamia. Published September 2018 by Captivating History. ASIN: B07HKXNR6W

Blackaby, H.T., & King, C.V.K. (2004). *Experiencing God: Knowing and doing the will of God.* Nashville: Broadman & Holman.

Bonhoeffer, Dietrich (1959). *The Cost of Discipleship.* Published by SCM Press Ltd.

Brueggemann, William (2007). *Praying the Psalms: Engaging Scripture and the Life of the Spirit.* Cascade Books.

Cloud, Dr. H., & Townsend, J. (1992). *Boundaries.* Grand Rapids: Zondervan Publishing House.

Deen, E. (1955). *All of the Women of the Bible.* New York: Harper & Row.

DeHaan, Mart (1999). *Our Daily Bread.* Discovery House Publishers.

Evans, A.T. (2005). *Let it Go: Breaking free from fear and anxiety.* Chicago: Moody.

Franklin, J. (2008). *Fasting: Opening the door to a deeper, more intimate, more powerful relationship with God.* Lake Mary, FL: Charisma House.

Kuykendall, C. (1955, 2000). *Loving and Letting Go: The Key to Being a Good Mom.* Grand Rapids: Zondervan.

Lutzer, E. (2000). *Getting closer to God: Keys to spiritual intimacy from the life of Moses.* Ann Arbor: Servant Publications.

Miller, Stephen M. (2007). The Complete Guide to the Bible. Uhrichsville, Ohio: Barbour Publishing, Inc.

Morris, Henry Madison (1985). *Biblical Basis for Modern Science.* Grand Rapids. Baker Publishing Group

Ortlund, A. (1977, 1984). *Disciplines of a Beautiful Woman.* Waco, TX: Word.

Petersen, Eugene H. (2002) *The Message Bible.* Published by NavPress.

Smalley, G. & Trent, J. (1990, 1992). *The Two Sides of Love: Twenty specific ways to build unbreakable bonds with your family and friends.* Irving, TX: Word.

Spurgeon, Charles H. (1997). *Spurgeon's Sermon Notes: Over 250 Sermons Including Notes, Commentary and Illustrations by Charles H. Spurgeon.* Published by Hendrickson Publishers Marketing, LLC

The Complete Book of Hymns: Inspiring Stories About 600 Hymns And Praise Songs by William J. Petersen & Ardythe Petersen. Published by Tyndale House Publishers, Inc. 2006.

Wilkinson, T. J.; Wilkinson, E. B.; Ur, J.; Altaweel, M. (2005). "Landscape and Settlement in the Neo-Assyrian Empire". *Bulletin of the American Schools of Oriental Research.*

Wilson, P.B. (1990). Liberated *Through Submission: The Ultimate Paradox.* Eugene, OR: Harvest House.

Wright, Paul H., Ph.D. (2012). *Rose then and Now bible Map Atlas with Biblical Background and Culture.* Rose publishing.

How to Know God

Did you know that you were created to have a loving relationship with God? He is patiently and lovingly waiting for you to respond to His invitation to salvation. Yes, you can receive forgiveness for your sins and assurance of eternal life through faith in His only Son, the Lord Jesus Christ.

> God so loved the world that He gave His only begotten Son, that whoever believes in Him should not perish but have everlasting life. For God did not send his Son into the world to condemn the world, but that the world through Him might be saved.
> John 3:16-17 (NKJV)

> "Now this is eternal life, that they may know You, the only true God, and Jesus Christ whom You have sent" (John 17:3).

You may be asking yourself *How can I know God?* Man is able to know the true and living God through His Word (that is, the Bible). The Bible reveals God's character and His plan for mankind. It is through reading His Word that we come to a knowledge of the righteousness of God and that which He requires of us.

What is it that prevents us from personally knowing God? Our sin has separated us from God. Our corruption is to such a degree that we cannot know Him personally and cannot experience His love. God's Word says, "All have sinned and fall short of the glory of God" (Romans 3:23). Man was created to have fellowship with God, but because of his sin (anything that is against the righteousness revealed in God's Law) he is prevented from that fellowship. This includes anything less than perfect obedience to God's commands.

"The wages of sin is death" (Romans 6:23a). The ultimate result of this death is an eternity in Hell. This spiritual death forces a separation from God. Man is sinful and God is holy. This creates a gulf unbridgeable by man making that intended fellowship impossible. The only solution is a divine bridge—that bridge is Christ.

God created a way by sending His Son to pay the price for our sin. "God demonstrated His own love toward us, in that while we were still sinners, Christ died for us" (Romans 5:8). He died in our place; He who knew no sin became sin for us. This removed our burden of sin and allows us to enter into that desired fellowship if we follow His way.

He is the only way. Jesus said, "I am the way, the truth, and the life. No one comes to the Father except through Me" (John 14:6).

It is not just enough that you know these truths. We must individually place our trust in Jesus Christ as our Lord and Savior. It is by repenting of our sins and believing on Christ that we can know God personally and experience His love.

> "But as many as receive Him, to them He gave the right to become children of God, to those who believe in His name" (John 1:12).

> For by grace you have been saved through faith, and that not of yourselves; it is the gift of God, not of works, lest anyone should boast. For we are His workmanship, created in Christ Jesus for good

works, which God prepared beforehand that we should walk in them
> Ephesians 2:8-10

"Repent, and let every one of you be baptized in the name of Jesus Christ for the remission of sins; and you shall receive the gift of the Holy Spirit" (Acts 2:38).

You can receive Jesus Christ right now by faith.

If you confess with your mouth the Lord Jesus and believe in your heart that God has raised Him from the dead, you will be saved. For with the heart, one believes unto righteousness, and with the mouth confession is made to salvation
> Romans 10:9-10

If you now believe on God and place your faith in His Son, congratulations and welcome to His family. We, all being His children, share in a heavenly inheritance! We are heirs to heaven and are promised the eternal pleasure of glorifying God. As our life here on earth progresses, God will continue to work in our hearts. We are daily being conformed to the image of Christ. We will begin to live lives of righteousness. Obedience to God will not be a burden to us, but rather a joy.

You may wonder now that you are a Christian, "What now?" For believers, new and old, it is fourfold: 1) find a church so you might hear the preaching of the Word and rejoice in the fellowship of other Christians, 2) study the Bible for that is where we learn of God and His plans, 3) pray to Him to strengthen your faith and increase your love toward Him, and 4) enjoy the blessings given by God in the heavenly ordained sacraments: baptism and the Lord's Supper. All of these will work to encourage and build upon your faith. If you have any questions, search the Scriptures or ask your pastor.

    http://www.blueletterbible.org/knowgod.cfm

Lavern - Papanui

1pm   12 noon → 1p